# A GUIDE TO

# WELLBEING

## *from the inside out*

PUBLISHING

## Hazel Boylan

A GUIDE TO WELLBEING *from the inside out*
Copyright © Hazel Boylan 2019
ISBN 978-1-912328-35-2
http://www.HazelBoylan.com

*Orla Kelly Publishing,*
*27 Kilbrody, Mount Oval,*
*Rochestown, Cork.*

# Disclaimer

This book has been written for self-care and educational purposes. The author is not offering it as a substitute for professional and qualified health, nutritional or lifestyle advice. It does not offer any guarantees and assumes no liability of any kind in respect to the accuracy or completeness of its contents. The author shall not be held liable or responsible to any person or entity with regard to issues of mental, physical or general health or wellbeing. Nor to any consequential physical, mental or general health issues alleged to have been caused directly or indirectly by the information or content of this book.

A GUIDE TO WELLBEING *from the inside out*

by Hazel Boylan

To Ger

and

Pierre, Michaela (RIP), Ruby, Robyn, Tadhg and Ellie

# Acknowledgements

A very special and heartfelt appreciation to Val Freeman in her role as beta-reader and sounding-board, while keeping me on track with grammatical and stylistic guidance. Her steer on expressing ideas more sensitively made a significant difference to this book.

Also to Brona Donnelly for her thorough appraisal and feedback – many thanks.

Gratitude to Rachel Donnelly (no relation to Brona) for editorial guidance in helping to bring coherence to early drafts.

My heartfelt thanks to Longtable Writers Brian Grehan, Paddy Hayes, Cole Jennings, Sandra MacCowen, Seán O'Hara, Yvonne Sheerin and Valerie Wade for their valuable and ever-insightful feedback on the many chapters.

To Susie Shelmerdine, author of *Your EFT Business*, for allowing me to reproduce a case study. And to the clients whose names and details have been changed for reasons of privacy, but whose stories appear in these pages.

# Contents

Disclaimer ........................................................................iii

Acknowledgements.........................................................vii

Introduction...................................................................xi

**Section 1 The Brain** ................................................... 1

1 Brain........................................................................3

2 Brain Health.............................................................15

**Section 2 Relationships**................................................ 33

3 Assertiveness ...........................................................35

4 Personal Boundaries ..................................................51

5 Communicating and Influencing.....................................63

6 Anger and Trauma......................................................71

7 DIY Life Coaching......................................................81

**Section 3 Mind**............................................................ 95

8 The Learning Process..................................................97

9 Change Starts with the Mind .......................................109

10 Comfort Zones and Effectiveness.................................119

11 Motivation.............................................................131

12 Reality .................................................................143

13 Science and Mind ....................................................151

14 Healthcare under the Microscope .................................159

15 The Energy Body .....................................................169

16 Emotional Freedom Technique.....................................177

17 Getting Down to Tapping............................................187

18 Matrix Reimprinting.................................................203

**Section 4 Spirituality** ................................................................**213**

Body and soul ....................................................................215

About the Author....................................................................227

Please Review this Book .............................................................229

Recommended TED Talks and YouTube Videos ............................231

Index ....................................................................................241

Bibliography.........................................................................253

Endnotes ..............................................................................255

# Introduction

This is a self-help book. **Its intention is to provide information that will shine a light on wellbeing as a process, introduce new ways to grow in potential and feel comfortable while doing so.** My belief, and the premise underlying the topics addressed in each chapter, is the indisputable fact of the mind-body connection, and our ability to influence it. Meaning that our thoughts, feelings, beliefs and attitudes positively or negatively affect how we show up in our lives. If this is an unfamiliar concept, then this book might be just what you need.

Readers of books in the self-help genre usually end up doing one of two things: going out and buying another after they've finished the last, or getting off their butts and their untapped potential with the intention of changing and flourishing. All of the millions of words carry more or less the same message: how to move from where you are to where you want to be. A thousand roadmaps. A thousand destinations. A thousand ways to get there. Some are practical guides. Some promote a specific methodology. Some are more persuasive than others.

Buckminster Fuller (1895–1983) was the second World President of Mensa[1] who broke the mould when he said something like, 'There's no use trying to change human nature. It's been the same for a very long time. Instead, go after the tools. New tools make new practices. Better tools make better practices.' In today's world, these tools are not the steam engine or chain saw, but information: the Internet, books, new thinking, new science, understanding brain processes and complementary healing methods.

Regard this book as a tool. Some of the concepts you may find hard to believe, challenging or downright controversial. All have been well-tested by practitioners in their fields, medical and other professionals who have discovered new paradigms in health and wellbeing.

Wellbeing[i] isn't about feeling happy, or having enough money, or being your ideal weight. *A GUIDE TO WELLBEING from the inside out* uses the model suggested by Daniel Siegel's Triangle of Well-being, incorporating **brain** function, the **mind**'s psychological and emotional terrain, and the importance of **relationships**, not in isolation, but as interdependent parts. Wellbeing is 'wholebeing', living in balance and harmony. This triangle informs the structure of the book, with chapters organised into Section 1 Brain, Section 2 Mind, and Section 3 Relationships.

Already I can hear some of you ask, 'But what about Spirituality? Where does it fit in?' Take a triangle, and in your mind turn it into a 3D pyramid. Integrating the three aspects of whole-brain functioning to form the apex takes us into the realm of spirituality or transcendence. Section 4 is Spirituality.

*A GUIDE TO WELLBEING from the inside out* illustrates the need to get our act together with conscious attention. It is about keeping multiple balls in the air in a controlled and practised way. Getting the disparate parts of our brain working as a team, ensuring the mind is house-trained in good and positive habits, that relationships are supportive, nurturing and fun, and committing to matters beyond ourselves in altruistic and spiritual ways are the threads that weave together the fabric of this book. When all are in balance, we are buoyant and resilient, and we thrive.

As a student of Psychology at Trinity College, Dublin, I undertook a project using a before-and-after model whereby hospital patients learned to improve heart rate and stress levels while attached to

---

i - Siegel's Triangle of Well-being is hyphenated. Elsewhere wellbeing is one word.

biofeedback equipment while using relaxation techniques. The purpose was to empower patients to self-manage pain or stress. My career since that time has dwelt much on how to engage our own resources to lead more meaningful and fulfilled lives using the empowered self.

This is an era when advances in quantum physics, neuroscience, technology, spirituality, complementary healing methods and psychology are merging. Touching on all of these, this book is a starting point for individuals to ask questions and discover new continents: to understand what lies behind old habits, thoughts and behaviours, one action, one disappointment, one failure or success at a time. In other words, it is a guide to assist the reader to discover new pathways to personal growth. An accredited STEPS to Excellence for Personal Success trainer for many years, trainees frequently asked me why the course I delivered was not available more widely. This book incorporates a wider range of personal development topics as an attempt to offer a taster of the growth potential we can tap into, with ideas for further exploration. Each chapter touches on a process I have used in some form or other; chapters are not exhaustive, but rather digestible introductions to ideas and techniques. A list of TED Talks intended to expand this information is available at the end of the book.

As the saying goes, there are many ways up the mountain: this book is one.

# Section 1 The Brain

Parallels are frequently drawn between the brain and a computer. There are positives and negatives to this that are easy to understand, with some differences. A computer can be switched off, while switching off the brain is virtually impossible. To fix a computer requires new parts or new software. While new parts are not available for the brain, we can upgrade the software and hardware by changing our habitual thinking and behaviour patterns. Technologists can expand a computer memory by adding a card. The brain's capacity to upgrade or downgrade is more subtle and happens consciously and unconsciously. What computers lack is imagination, the ability to interpret the world or come up with new ideas. Brains, by comparison, can create rainbows out of teardrops. Or instruments so amazing they can measure light or the heartbeat of a flea. Or spaceships that can orbit the moon and the stars and travel to other worlds.

This section looks at the structure of the brain and specific measures to keep it healthy.

# 1 Brain

*The human brain has 100 billion neurons, each neuron connected to 10 thousand other neurons. Sitting on your shoulders is the most complicated object in the known universe.'* This quote from American theoretical physicist and populariser of science, Michio Kaku, puts into context the extraordinary and complex nature of this organ – the brain.

The non-stop activity of the organ inside our heads is fascinating and complex. This chapter will go some way toward explaining and simplifying some of its functions, and how we can use this information to our advantage. Some of the gains we make by being aware of brain function can be as quick as 'add water and stir'. Others come more slowly as some of our behaviours were learned and embedded in ways we may believe are unchangeable, and therefore more difficult to shift. Behaviour and beliefs that are learned are second nature. Anything learned can be unlearned. With awareness and time, practice and persistence we can exercise choice to upgrade these and…voilà! transformation.

The job of our brain is to help us make sense of the world, to remember, learn, plan, concentrate and have a clear, active mind. On top of these *thinking* aspects, and all the things we have learned, are the vital brain functions we take for granted: breathing, heartbeat and digestive processes. For the purposes of this chapter, it is the thinking and learning parts of our brain on which we will focus.

The brain is not a single unit. It is made up of parts or sections, made up of neurons which vaguely resemble a tree. Dendrites and axons, like the branches and the roots of the tree, are the parts that transmit signals. The brain, containing billions of nerve cells, thus connects at more than 100 trillion points. Scientists call this dense, branching network a 'neuron forest'.[2] Signals that form memories and thoughts move through an individual neuron and connect with others as tiny electrical charges. Connections in the forest form associations, which deliver our experience of the world. It is when these signals are interrupted through disease, tumour or acquired brain injury that memory loss or other disability occurs.

Every brain is different, even those of identical twins. The brain processes information according to programmes, rules, filters and associations learned through experience and upbringing. Previously understood to be a static organ that deteriorated with age, advances in brain science and neuroscience have radicalised our understanding of what goes on inside our heads.[3]

Microscopic changes and remapping of the brain – the forming and norming of structural and functional circuits through repetition – is down to the remarkable feature known as brain plasticity: its ability to grow, prune and change according to the experience and learning to which it is exposed. It is this exciting and relatively newly-understood feature, the brain's plasticity, that is the platform for personal growth.

## Dominant Brain Functions

The brain has many specialised systems that work across specific regions to help us talk, make sense of what we see, recognise objects and help solve problems. For reasons of simplicity, what follows is an introduction to how just some of these parts process information.

Just as we have two fully-functioning hands capable of all manner of motor coordination, yet default to the dominant hand for the majority of actions, so, too, do we have brain activity to which we default. To extend the analogy of hand dominance, we have the ability to write or brush our teeth with the non-dominant hand, but because it takes

4

effort and concentration and a learning curve we may be too impatient to endure, it is often easier to give up and rely on the one that feels most comfortable. The dominant hand becomes so practiced that it can perform most things automatically. In the same way, our brain has become so practiced in the way it takes in and processes information, that we are convinced by the template of our own story.

## Left and Right Brains

A good starting point is to understand the architecture of the brain and how it influences us.

The largest part of the brain, the cerebrum, is divided into two hemispheres, left and right. The illustration below shows a bird's eye view of the brain with left and right hemispheres, which control the body's motor activity: the left controls the right side of the body and the right controls the left side.

The architecture of the brain controlling opposite sides of the body means that trauma such as stroke or an acquired brain injury to the left brain will impair the right side of the body and *vice versa*.

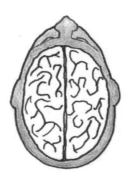

**Cross-section of brain showing left and right hemispheres**

5

In addition, and more important for understanding ourselves, left and right brain *functions* are also quite distinct and are outlined below.

| Left Brain Function | Right Brain Function |
|---|---|
| — Processes information in a linear manner | — Is holistic |
| — Identifies important details | — Picks up and interprets non-verbal signals - body language |
| — Is analytical and likes order | — Sees the big picture |
| — Works to sequence information | — Is visceral, trusting gut and heart feelings |
| — Uses logic to solve problems | — Is intuitive and influenced by the meaning and feeling of an experience |
| — Is influenced by higher-order thinking | |
| — Applies the letter of the law | — Interprets the spirit of the law |
| — Likes structure | — Uses symbols, metaphor and context |
| — Is literal and unambiguous | |
| — Values the grammar and syntax of language | — Uses expression and the poetry of language |

Even though there is ongoing communication between the hemispheres, as with handedness, brain dominance means that an individual has a natural preference for processing information using one side of the brain over the other. The right side is considered the intuitive, creative or spontaneous side, while the left is the logical, linear, structured side.

The left brain is the predominant hemisphere engaged through most of our years at school. This happens because the majority of schools regard the brain primarily as an information storage and retrieval system which rewards accurate recall, order, grammar, multiplication tables and facts. When a system focuses on the detail such as getting correct answers, bigger-picture thinking, curiosity and creativity are downgraded and we lose the ability to develop associations – a function of the right brain. The soft skills of confidence, motivating self and others, resilience, attitude, goal-setting, beliefs, creativity, managing change, self-esteem and self-management habits, the domain of the right brain, enjoy far less attention in the race for top marks.

The corpus callosum is a broad band of nerve fibres that link left and right hemispheres, allowing information, emotions and reason to mingle. Optimal learning occurs when both left and right brains share and balance function. When both halves are connected and integrated, we experience sound mental health and a sense of wellbeing.

Balanced functioning, in Buddhist thinking known as the 'Middle Way', is like a boat trip down a river. One bank, the left brain, is specific and rigid – it offers no soft landing. It is the territory of inflexibility and dictatorship. The opposite bank represents the absence of boundaries or structure. It is the territory of no boundaries, no structure and breakdown, creating an environment of chaos. The challenge for the boatman is to steer a middle course – not veering too close to either bank for fear of being overwhelmed by one extreme or the other.

Left and right brains working as a team are said to be **horizontally integrated**. If we are dominated by either one or the other, we are living in an emotional desert or in raging disorder. Integrating left and right hemispheres[4] brings us back to the zone of effortlessness, and we are once more *in the flow*.

A real-life account of the structural breakdown of the brain can be found online. Brain scientist Dr Jill Bolte Taylor describes a research opportunity few in her profession would wish for: she had a massive stroke, and watched as her brain functions — motion, speech, self-awareness — shut down. She explains the parallel worlds of left and right brain functioning in her story, *My Stroke of Insight*, referenced in the TED Talks listed at the end.

## Upstairs and Downstairs Brains

The cortex, the upstairs brain, is the newest part in evolutionary terms. It regards itself as the captain of the brain team because it has the power to know what we think, feel and do. Its purpose is to understand, use language, plan and express thoughts – higher-order thinking. When the upstairs brain is functioning well, we are more in control, think before we act and regulate our emotions. The upstairs brain is the orchestrator of healthy functioning.

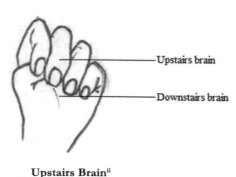

**Upstairs Brain**[ii]

The upstairs brain surrounds the downstairs brain like a fist. The upstairs prefrontal cortex is the intentional, thinking, planning part of our brain that allows us to make good decisions, plan ahead, exercise moral judgement, be able to understand past and future, and control our emotions. It can delay pleasure and predict the future result of actions

Continually growing throughout childhood and into our twenties, the upstairs brain goes through a major remodel during adolescence.

ii - Hand Model of the Brain is adapted with permission from page 20 of the book The Developing Mind: How Relationships and the Brain Interact to Shape Who We Are (2nd Ed) by Daniel J. Siegel (Guildford, 2012)

The downstairs brain is the thumb and palm in the fist model, and is made up of different parts. It functions as the alarm system, our fight, flight or freeze survival mechanism, as well as acting as the storehouse of our emotions.

The downstairs brain is with us at birth and never leaves us. It is the part of our brain that keeps us breathing, keeps our heart beating, and keeps other basic systems – those we cannot do without – functioning.

The downstairs brain is the storehouse of emotion – the ones we take pleasure in such as love and passion, as well as the scary emotions we try to avoid: anger, fear, guilt and frustration, among others.

Let me be clear: there is nothing negative about strong emotions like anger. Emotions fulfil their purpose by providing us with vital information. It is *how we deal with them* that is critical. To recognise and express love or anger appropriately is a sign of emotional maturity, a healthy practice in the ongoing management of our lives and our relationships. It happens when the captain of the brain team is in charge, and when the brain is **vertically integrated**. If we inappropriately express or swallow corrosive emotions we fail ourselves and others. This is what gives anger, in particular, its bad press. There is more on anger in chapter 6.

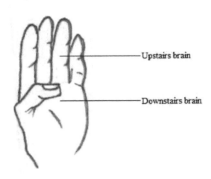

Upstairs brain

Downstairs brain

**Downstairs Brain Flipping its Lid**

When triggered to react by a real or perceived threat, the evolutionarily reactive, downstairs brain takes over. With fingers open, it has 'flipped its lid'. It communicates spontaneously and is in charge of our defences, taking all measures necessary for survival. When threatened, we abandon the slower, higher processing brain and succumb to the emotional, reactive brain. Its motto is: act now, think later.

We do not make good decisions when the emotional brain is in charge. The metaphor of a baby-gate between the upstairs and downstairs brains helps us understand. Learning to manage the baby gate to monitor the downstairs brain, to shift from reactive to proactive mode, keeps our emotions in check. Vertical integration is managing our reactivity, understanding where it is coming from and expressing it appropriately.

| Upstairs Brain | Downstairs Brain |
|---|---|
| – Thoughtful, considered action<br>– Sound decision making and planning<br>– Control over emotions and body<br>– Self-understanding<br>– Empathy and compassion<br>– Morality – doing what's right | – Instinct, gut-reaction<br>– Breathing, blinking, innate reactions, impulses (fight, flight, freeze) and strong emotions (e.g. anger and fear)<br>– Survival and basic necessities |

When horizontal and vertical integration is achieved, upstairs and downstairs, left and right brains, all in balance at the same time, we experience whole-brain functioning.

Understanding these crucial characteristics helps us to achieve a state of brain harmony that will allow change and growth in undreamed of ways.

Dr. Robert Resnick, a psychotherapist in Los Angeles, provides an easy formula to help understand the process of reactivity and how we can move away from reactivity to more mindful brain functioning.

$$\text{Event} + \text{Response} = \text{Outcome}$$
$$E + R = O$$

In the sequence of things, an Event (E) occurs – something happens beyond our control and we Respond (R). This produces an Outcome (O). When something happens we may pass through it without consequence or we may be affronted. It is either resolved and integrated, or remains unresolved and is logged as a reference point marked 'alert'. The trouble is that unresolved issues accumulate and calcify and are often referred to as our 'personal baggage'. It is the unspent residue of the emotional brain that clouds our options and limits our outcomes.

## An example from real life. . .

... it was a fine sunny morning on my walk, when the screech of brakes warned me of a nearby cyclist as we approached a busy intersection. Suddenly there was a woman standing in her dressing gown and pyjamas, arms on hips, berating the cyclist for disturbing her sleep; she had been lurking behind the garden gate waiting for just this moment. 'So it's you with the brakes! You wake me up every morning with the screech of them'. The cyclist may or may not have responded, but pedalled away. I was amused by the event and remarked that she must already have been awake. 'I am entitled to some peace in my own home', she barked, 'he wakes me up every morning! Every morning he disturbs my sleep', the start to her day ruined. 'All I want is some peace!'

The event (E) – the squeaky brakes – is something beyond her control that she can do nothing about. She reacts with annoyance (R) which ruins the start to her day (O), the adrenaline keeping her body charged long after the event is over.

| Squeaky brakes | + | Annoyance | = | Frustration/anger/ ruined day |
|---|---|---|---|---|
| E | + | R | = | O |

Her frustration and anger and my momentary amusement were two quite different outcomes. So it is not the event, but how we interpret it, that is the issue. When we react mindlessly we forfeit the choice to think and act in our own best interests. It is in the fractional space between E and R where opportunity for change lies. The only part of the equation we have control over is R – how we react. Once we realise that we have the ability to hit the pause button, take a moment to open communications between our left and right, upstairs and downstairs brains, we are free to consider alternatives. When we take charge of that split second before R, we have closed the baby-gate and freed up the potential for change. Instead of being driven by her fight response, she might, instead, have snuggled under her duvet and relished the comfort of her bed while thinking of others on their way to work.

## Integration – Whole-Brain Functioning

Growing up most people have experienced rivalry, tantrums, disobedience, homework battles or other disciplinary matters, occasions when the downstairs, left or right brains were in charge – all instances illustrating the absence of whole-brain functioning. When one aspect is vying for dominance over the others, either within the individual or between two people, a stand-off or win-lose situation arises.

When disagreements happen, it helps to pause and take note from which part of the brain you are operating. It is likely that the other person is using the opposite side to the one you are using. Once the left side of your brain has divorced itself from feelings and personal experience, the domain of the right, it is locked into rigidity. No logic or reason will prevail and no settlement will be reached.

Knowledge of the pause button gives you the potential to step out of the rut that has you branded as a resistance fighter. Once you are able to convey to the other that you understand their point of view, you have moved into the place of integration. The chances are that your opponent will reduce their resistance. But even if they do not, you have stepped away from a wrestling match that rarely ends in a draw: there is usually a winner and a loser or two losers.

And the exciting thing is this: opportunities to learn whole-brain integration occur when we are faced with challenges. Brain plasticity, the wondrous ability of the brain to grow new connections and prune others, means we can methodically deconstruct the superhighways of habits that no longer serve us by pressing the pause button between E and R. With the captain of the brain team now in charge, we can replace our ineffective thoughts and beliefs to form new and improved attitudes and habits. The notion of wellbeing is real and within our grasp.

# 2 Brain Health

In matters of brain health, as with the rest of the body with its disparate systems, organs and parts, what everyone hopes for and aspires to is optimal wellbeing. We all know there is a body-mind connection – think of the placebo effect – but there is also a body-brain connection. You may well ask what is the difference between mind and brain? The mind is the processing of thoughts and experiences – the psychological aspect of our lives. The brain, like the stomach, spleen or heart, is the matter, the organ made of tissue requiring a healthy blood supply, oxygen and nutrition. Brain health, then, is the degree to which we put in place those aspects that optimise brain matter and reduce or eliminate those that impair it.

Brain health and positive mental health are travelling companions, meaning that educators, physicians and holistic health practitioners who seek to promote mental, emotional and social health are on the same page. We know that mental disorders are brain disorders from evidence of changes in the anatomy, physiology and chemistry of the nervous system.[5] When the brain cannot effectively coordinate the billions of cells in the body, the results impact many aspects of life.

Like physical health, brain health to large degree, is a lifestyle choice: it requires exercise, specific and proper nutrition, cognitive activity and social engagement to reduce the risk of memory deterioration as we grow older.[6]

Academic and media interest in brain health is global and current, so much so that Trinity College Dublin's Institute of Neuroscience, in partnership with the University of California, San Francisco have established the Global Brain Health Institute that will train 600 students in brain health, its first intake having been in 2016.[7] Focusing primarily on dementia, this scientific project will look at preventive measures from a multi-disciplinary viewpoint, including lifestyle, dietary, cognitive and exercise decisions as global imperatives for healthier aging populations. Medicating as treatment is no longer regarded as inevitable; prevention and reversal of conditions are being pursued as superior outcomes.

Neuroscientists have shown that the brain and body are intricately tied, where a healthy body equals a healthy brain. Exercise, social connection and keeping the brain active with three measures, challenge, change and learning, are crucial to avoid cognitive decline.[8]

- **Challenge.** Satisfaction from doing things slightly beyond your comfort zone actually changes brain chemistry, the stretch creating a sense of positivity. Mental puzzles and physical challenges are inextricably linked with brain health. Indeed, physical exercise produces a protein which is the equivalent of brain fertilizer[iii] that encourages the growth of new connections and brain cells. This is why we are encouraged to take thirty minutes of physical exercise, like walking, at least five times a week.

- **Change.** This could be anything in your lifestyle: diet, activity, novelty, making that phone call to friends or family. Surprise yourself: make fresh choices, take a different route to work, choose to cook a meal with fresh produce and invite friends to share it, read a book you would normally overlook, learn about nutrition, decide to meditate regularly. Experiment widely and wildly. Have fun, surprise yourself.

- **Learn something new.** Explore a topic in which you are interested but have little knowledge, or take on an activity you have never done before, like juggling or playing bridge. Learning en-

---

iii    BDNF - Brain-derived neurotrophic factor

courages the growth of brain cells and stimulates connections, which is hugely beneficial, because stronger brain connections support brain health.

We talk about the brain as if it were a single unit, matter that fills the skull with a host of jobs to keep us functioning. But as with any complex organ, we also know that some parts, or all, can let us down: we can suffer brain fog, have difficulty in focussing, suffer memory loss or numerous other conditions including psychological and neurological issues, depression, Alzheimer's and Parkinson's disease.[9]

Until twenty or so years ago, experts considered the brain a finite organ which peaked at around age twenty five, and then began to decline with no possibility of reprieve. However, science now tells us that the brain is an organ in constant flux, generating new cells and growing and pruning neural connections in dynamic ways depending on the environment until the day we die.[10] The brain's ability to change is called plasticity. As with any muscle, the brain responds through a range of factors which aid and abet its viability or deterioration, especially as we age; in other words, the belief that the brain is on a predictable and downward trajectory has been quashed. The metaphor of the brain as a machine or computer has done us something of a disservice, for we now know we are not limited by the brain we were born with, but have within our power the potential to upgrade its health, or, indeed let it deteriorate. It is within each individual's remit to take it in either direction.

We brush our teeth twice a day, floss, and regularly attend the dentist. Unlike dental health, brain health is something most of us do little to consciously manage, simply because our knowledge about it is minimal. When we enjoy brain health, brain and mind are coherent and we experience a sense of free-flow in our lives, we are mentally alert and know who we are and what purpose we serve. We are resilient, cope well with stress and are in charge of our actions. We remember names and facts, can recall the past and envisage the future. We can plan and execute, follow up or follow through. Life is good.

The absence of brain health hampers us. Our mental acuity may be fuzzy, or we may experience mood swings, inattention, panic, sleep problems, depression or suicidal thoughts, all conditions suggesting the brain is below par.[11] Brain health, then, fluctuates on a continuum from high functioning to severe debilitation and can include psychological, neurological, physiological, immunological or trauma issues.

## Brain-Gut Connection

Our gastrointestinal (GI) tract or gut is a very large sensory organ. Can you believe that if all the folds and protrusions were stretched out it would be between 30 and 40 square meters? It is somewhat smaller than original calculations equalling the size of a tennis court, but nevertheless is a large and critical aspect of our physiology.[12] It collects information - not only relating to the quality of nutrients, but hormonal mixes, toxicities and other invaders. The GI tract contributes a lot to processing emotions and awareness, and gauging how the whole body is doing.[13] In other words, the GI tract is not just the conveyor of food through the body, but is inextricably bound to our emotional wellbeing.

We have all experienced *butterflies in the stomach* or *trusted our gut* — signals that alert us to certain conditions in our environment. The GI tract (the oesophagus, stomach, small and large intestines and colon) is an open-ended but closed, contained system. The GI tract comprises a lining of nerve cells, with its own set of neurotransmitters for sending messages, and also has the ability to learn and remember.[14] The brain and the gut are connected by the vagus nerve, which are in constant two-way communication along this nerve pathway, called the gut-brain axis. [15] What the gut-brain axis tells us is that everything is connected. Everything we do, think, eat, how we sleep and live, stressed or calm, can affect the brain. Our entire body – all the systems, independent and closed as they are, are constantly interacting. The gut is not capable of thought, but is involved in letting the brain know of any unwanted threats from the environment or from what we eat. Indeed, the gut talks to the brain much more than the other way round, where 90% of information is delivered from gut to the brain, with only 10% the other way round. What the brain does is make sense of the information supplied by the gut. [16]

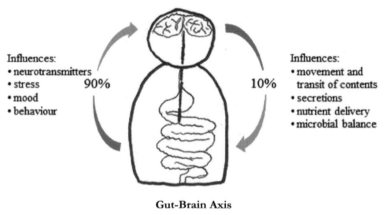

Influences:
• neurotransmitters
• stress          90%
• mood
• behaviour

Influences:
• movement and
   transit of contents
• secretions
• nutrient delivery
• microbial balance

10%

**Gut-Brain Axis**

## Leaky Brain

The tragic part of debilitation or, in its extreme case, what Dr Mark Hyman calls *broken brain,* is that we frequently feel the slide down the slippery slope from which there is little chance of escape. [17]

Blood vessels delivering oxygen and nutrients to the brain cross the blood-brain barrier. This is a specialised system like a micro-fine sieve that protects the brain from toxins circulating in the blood. A compromised blood-brain barrier leads to leaky brain syndrome. Disruption of the blood-brain barrier, making it permeable to toxins, pathogens and other potentially dangerous substances, can cause headaches, cognitive decline, chronic fatigue syndrome and neurological disorders.[18] The good news is that the brain has the ability to bounce back. By addressing lifestyle, nutrition, dietary, social, sleep and exercise regimes, we can hop off the rollercoaster ride.

An action that costs nothing but the choice to go to bed earlier, sleep regulates the functions and integrity of the blood brain barrier. The Nobel Prize in Physiology or Medicine in 2017 was awarded for research on circadian rhythms, the cycle that governs the body's clock of sleep and wakefulness. With expert precision, our inner clock regulates functions such as behaviour, hormone levels, sleep, body temperature and metabolism. Our brain function and, in turn, our wellbeing is affected when there is a temporary mismatch between our external environment and our internal biological clock.[19] Going to bed later than we should is the equivalent of self-imposed jet lag. When we deprive ourselves of the healing cycles of REM sleep, we are prescribing ill-health.[20] The brain as a living, pulsing organ responds kindly to the care we afford it by halting, and in many cases, restoring brain function.[21]

## Broken Brain

Telling his own story, Dr Mark Hyman was a successful medical practitioner, able to remember patients and their histories and engage with them in a friendly and confident manner.[22] He was athletic: cycling a hundred miles in a day was a cinch. Almost overnight he went from full health to barely being able to walk up the stairs: he was disoriented and terrified. He had muscle pain and twitches, insomnia, digestive problems, food allergies, depression and anxiety, and was no longer interested in his patients. Specialists diagnosed chronic fatigue syndrome, which meant nothing other than that he felt chronically tired and out of sorts. He was prescribed anti-antidepressants, anxiety and attention deficit disorder medications, none of which helped.

A chance lecture by a nutritional biochemist led him to discover high levels of mercury in his hair and urine. He realised that it was not his brain or mind that was at fault, but toxicity in his body. Now, when he sees patients with mercury levels of 30-40 nanograms per millilitre (ng/mL) he knows it is serious. As a result of years spent in China, his level of mercury burden was 187 ng/mL, which he stored because his body was unable to detoxify or eliminate it.

Realising that each system within the body impacts on every other, he determined to cleanse his body of toxins. Clearing the heavy metals and balancing his hormones was a slow process that needed managing by a professional. Releasing, for example heavy metals into a compromised system would further undermine the body's elimination processes. Instead, his body needed to be stabilised and fortified prior to elimination to optimise its resilience for maximum effect.

Heavy metals, like lead in the air we breath and mercury leaking from dental fillings, enter the bloodstream, tissue and brain and poison us. Knowing this, dentists across the EU by law will stop using amalgam fillings—which contain 50% liquid mercury—in pregnant and nursing women and children under the age of 15 in July 2018.[23] We are also exposed to astounding amounts of brain pollution from toxic chemicals and pesticides, as well as, for example, aluminium in common household products like Liquid Gaviscon, deodorants, foil wrap, and saucepans. If we take these toxins in more quickly than the body can eliminate them, the accumulation can destabilise physical and mental health.[24]

## Leaky Gut

While taken with a grain of salt by some physicians, intestinal permeability, more frequently referred to as leaky gut, is nevertheless a serious condition in which the lining of the small intestine becomes inflamed and damaged.

An analogy of leaky gut is like tiles in a shower sealed by grouting to render it waterproof. When the seal is broken and made permeable, we detect a leak. In our gut, intestinal tight junction membranes, like grouting, join together to form a barrier virtually impermeable to fluid.[25] Inflammation causes swelling which expands the membrane, creating microscopic gaps or holes in the tissue. These gaps or leaks, developed gradually over time, enable undigested food particles, toxic waste and bacteria to breach the intestinal wall and enter the blood stream. This is bad news because it carries its undesirable load to the rest of the body, including the brain, and is the cause of chronic inflammatory diseases.[26]

According to Hyman, the main inflammatory culprits that cause leaks in the gastrointestinal (GI) tract are stress, refined sugar, dairy and gluten.[27]

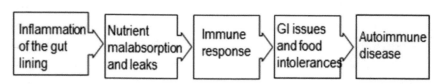

How a compromised gut impacts health and wellbeing

The cumulative effect of an inflammatory burden leads to compromised health and wellbeing, malabsorption and leaks. The body's defence team in the form of an immune response, if left unchecked, produces antibodies that end up attacking the body and brain as food intolerances or autoimmune disease or broken brain.[28]

A band aid applied to a leak serves no purpose if you continue to run the shower. In other words, medication alone (compounded by side-effects) treats only the symptom while ignoring the cause. The solution lies in managing and eliminating the source: stress, the food and toxins, and the body's inability to deal with them, that created the problem in the first place.

## The Microbiome

According to the revolution that is sweeping health research today, the missing piece connected to just about every disease is the microbiome.[29] A biome is a community of organisms that populate a habitat. In fact we have skin, oral, fecal and vaginal microbiomes as well as the one resident in the GI tract. Sometimes referred to as the 'second brain', the gut biome is roughly the same weight as the average human brain of 1.5 to 2 kg but carries multiple times greater genetic material than does the brain.[30]

The explosion of autoimmune disease worldwide, individuals (you and me) multiplied by millions upon millions, is a wake-up call. What actions can we take to reverse the threat of chronic conditions as a result of obsolete lifestyle habits? The time lag for microbiome awareness and inclusion in health education, textbooks and practitioner training could be as much as twelve years, according to Dr Pedram Shojai, far too long for the science to enter our health vocabulary. [31] It behoves us, then, to learn as much as we can about taking charge of our health and wellbeing, starting with the GI microbiome, both by informing ourselves and by seeking out general practitioners who are open to discussing a wider approach to health management.

Bacteria inhabiting the gut are so small they cannot be seen, but collectively are affected by, and in turn, affect whether or not your skin glows or your brain works. Within this population of trillions of gut bacteria are both good and bad, with a constant battle going on between them for dominance. Not to be underestimated, an imbalance in our gut biome, or dysbiosis, disrupts nutrient absorption and immune function, causes fatigue and can lead to chronic inflammatory disease.

Influenced largely by what we eat, our job is to consume a diet that supports the good bacteria to fight inflammation and disease. The balance tipped the other way causes us to crave the wrong foods and leads to aggravated dysbiosis – an imbalance between the types of organism present in the natural microflora – and a host of health problems. Undermining the gut biome, unavoidably, are the antibiotics in the food chain, the medications we take and the water we drink. Health and wellness rely on the promotion and predominance of good bacteria in the gut as a result of healthy food choices. This is also why a good quality, live yoghurt or other bioactive, fermented foods are recommended after a course of antibiotics to help repopulate the gut with beneficial bacteria.

Fergus Shanahan is Professor and Chair of the Department of Medicine at University College Cork, where his interest in GI health has defined him as a world-leader in the field. He created UCC's multi-disciplinary research Alimentary Pharmabiotic Centre, which is investigating how good gut bacteria can be used to promote brain health, general health and wellbeing.

Controlling for cause and effect, studies with mice have shown gut bacteria from obese mice transplanted into normal mice consuming a controlled diet quickly become obese. The opposite is true, too, where gut bacteria from normal mice transplanted into obese mice enable the obese subjects to lose weight. In other words, it is the quality of the gut biome that determines the outcome.[32]

Nor is this limited to body weight. Research has shown it applies to conditions such as cancer, cardiovascular disease, heart disease, depression and autism.[33]

Unpalatable as it may sound, researchers are discovering new human drug solutions by identifying the good bacteria from our gut, captured in our faeces.[34] Studies show that bacteria – both good and bad – send signals to the brain for our development and welfare. By identifying and isolating the good bacteria, smart antibiotics and new anti-inflammatory drugs have revolutionary potential for the food and pharmaceutical industries.

The gut microbiome thrives in the diversity of what we eat every day and is one of the drivers of our health trajectory. This is why we are encouraged to eat a rainbow diet of greens, reds, oranges, yellows and purples. (And, no, not m&m's). This advice is for everyone, but particularly in the elderly to beat frailty, susceptibility to inflammation, and infection and for their general health and wellbeing.[35]

## Serotonin, Dopamine and Melatonin

Brain health relies on powerful neurotransmitters, one of which is serotonin. This naturally occurring chemical is a contributor to feelings of contentment; it resists depression and other mood disorders. It is estimated that 90-95% percent of the body's serotonin is made in the GI tract.[36] Other neurotransmitters with important functions in the gut biome include dopamine and melatonin.[37] These support sleep regulation, cell and nerve function, and the immune system.[38] Researchers are finding evidence that irritation in the GI tract can also trigger mood changes. In other words, overall our gut health strongly indicates how we show up in our lives.

## Inflammation and Inflammatory Disease

If you banged your finger with a hammer or slammed it in a car door, it would swell, become inflamed, would not work well, and take a while to heal. Sending in the troops to mind the wound site is the body's natural defence team doing its job. We help the inflamed and painful finger by avoiding anything that would continue to harm it. Inflammation in the brain, gut, muscle, organ or joint has the same effect; it means that the organ is inflamed and cannot work efficiently. Once we aid the defence team by eliminating the cause of irritation, we set in motion the conditions for optimal healing.

More insidious, though, is when inflammation causes the disease, such as asthma, arthritis, inflammatory bowel and Crohn's disease. These more chronic inflammatory health conditions are the result of the immune system attacking the body's own cells or tissues.

One non-pharmaceutical approach for inflammatory diseases is through diet aiming to eliminate those foods that cause the inflammation.[39] Already mentioned is sugar. The Internet can provide as much information as is needed on inflammatory foods. Top of the list will invariably be what is called SAD, the Standard American Diet of highly processed food and refined sugar.

In Channel 4's *Sugar Rush* series (2015) by Jamie Oliver, his breakfast is overseen by a nutritionist who examined the *free sugar* count, that is refined sugar added to foods by the manufacturer. His breakfast was a bowl of bran flakes topped with milk, low fat yoghurt, a handful of blueberries and glass of orange juice – a healthy-sounding start to the day. Admittedly the nutritionist had picked the brand of orange juice with the highest sugar content, but Oliver was astonished to learn that the total free sugar content of his breakfast was 56.4 g or the equivalent of 14 teaspoons (5 teaspoons in his man-sized serving of bran flakes, 3 in the portion of yoghurt, 6 in the orange juice).

You may wonder why the blueberries as a source of sugar were not counted. Sugar Rush looked at sugar added during processing rather than natural sugars. Many people believe that because added sugars are bad, the same must apply to fruits, which contain fructose. However, this is a misconception. Fructose is harmful in large amounts, but it is almost impossible to overeat fructose by eating fruit alone. All berries are a good option for high-fiber, low-sugar fruits.

The idea behind eating your way to a healthy brain is to avoid or eliminate refined sugar and processed foods and increase the intake of fresh produce. The longer the processing journey and the more ingredients on the label, the greater the risk. We are encouraged to eat food as close to its natural state as possible, in other words, the less the processing, the better, as well as organic produce, without herbicides, pesticides and chemical additives, as healthier and safer choices.[40]

## Good food decisions

There is much debate about the healthier, nutritional superiority of organic produce. It has been shown that organic fruit and vegetables have superior antioxidant properties, which help protect the body from disease.[41] Plants absorb minerals from the soil. If the soil is depleted of minerals, the plant will suffer diminished nutritional value. Synthetic fertilizers deliver the primary nutrients needed for plant growth, but leave out the diverse micronutrients that lead to healthy soil. Even though organic farming cannot totally avoid contaminants through water leakage or airborne pollutants, organic methods maintain healthy soil by crop diversification, crop rotation and adding natural fertilizer such as manure or plant compost.[42] What is also recommended by many professional promoters of health is that we should move as close as we can to an 80% plant-based diet, rich in greens and multiple colours. Greens are packed with vitamins to support the body's repair and immune systems. They are important as a source of phytonutrients or natural chemicals, with great healing and nutritional properties. Greens are low in sugars and high in fibre which help regulate blood sugar levels. Each colour in fruits and vegetables is caused by specific chemicals that help protect plants from germs, insects, and other threats. And each colour indicates an abundance of specific nutrients that are beneficial to our overall health.[43]

## Bad food decisions

What does this mean for us? Evolution over millions of years created a human species digestively well adapted to dietary regimes best favoured by what was available to eat locally. But the majority of what we eat today differs grossly from that consumed by our ancestors.

From a production point of view it is hard to escape the results of corporate agribusiness, over-farming, depleted nutrients in soil augmented with chemical fertilizers and pesticides that end up in the food chain.

From a manufacturing point of view, processed, mass-produced, high-sugar carbohydrate foods with a long shelf life wreak havoc on the nutritional requirements of our bodies and brains. Colourants, flavour enhancers, additives, refining and bleaching are aspects of processing that add no nutritional benefit, while providing our bodies with elements they have not been designed to recognise, digest or absorb. The mismatch driven by what we consume is evident in the disease-and-obesity plague currently being experienced worldwide.[44]

In the last couple of hundred years we have been challenged with what has been summarised into seven crucial differences from that of our ancestors: 1) refined sugar load, 2) fatty acid composition, 3) high carbohydrate composition, 4) low mineral density, 5) acidic, 6) sodium-potassium ratio, and 7) fibre content. [45] This collision of our past with our present may underlie many of the chronic diseases of Western civilization.

Once associated with high-income countries, obesity and 'lifestyle diseases' are now also prevalent in low- and middle-income countries. These include deposits of fat in the arteries (atherosclerosis), heart disease and stroke, obesity and type 2 diabetes, and diseases associated with smoking, alcohol and drug abuse, hypertension, colon cancer, autoimmune disease and premature mortality.[46]

## Fat

For years we have been encouraged to go 'low-fat' in a bid to reduce cholesterol levels, the drive which spurred the development of low-fat options.

Tragically, and because our vocabulary has only one word for fat, this has added further to the confusion. But fats come in different forms – those that are good for us and those that are not. We are faced with labelling descriptions of fats as saturated, unsaturated, trans, hydrogenated, poly and mono-unsaturated. Little wonder we are confused. On the good side are the unsaturated fats, and those to avoid are the hydrogenated, trans- and saturated fats found in butter, dairy spreads, fatty meats, pastry, biscuits and cakes. Too much of the bad fats can increase our cholesterol, which increases health and disease risks.

## What about Gluten?

We have all seen footage of pizza chefs spinning and stretching dough, demonstrating its strength and elasticity. The ability of flour to stretch when water is added is due to the presence of gluten. In some of us the digestive tract can have difficulty breaking down the strength and elasticity of gluten for easy absorption into the bloodstream. Gut irritants such as this can cause inflammation, and, as we know, inflammation has an impact on our immune system with subsequent health issues.

A friend challenged me, saying that people have been consuming gluten for centuries. Yes, we have, but our ancestors were eating foods made from grains very different from those reaching the supermarket shelves today. While all have gluten, many products have fibres stripped and are made with hybrid grains sprayed with chemicals and pesticides that introduce other digestive and nutritional challenges. Our new generation, high-yield wheat varieties are treated in ways our ancestors could not have dreamed of.

In people diagnosed with coeliac disease or non-coeliac gluten sensitivity, even the smallest amount of gluten can have severe consequences. It is recognised now that people *without* coeliac disease also experience inflammation of the gut and a compromised gut biome.[47] Any level of inflammation has consequences for gut and brain health and sets the scene for immune conditions to flourish.

## Restoring Balance

In his book *The pH Miracle for Diabetes,* Young provides an easy-to-remember formula to restore the cycle of balance: the '3 Cs' towards wellbeing:

—  Stage 1: **Cleanse** the body from the inside out, eliminating the acid wastes from taking control with good quality water, green foods and green drinks.

—  Stage 2: **Control** negative habits of eating, thinking and living to break the pattern of disturbance.

—  Stage 3: **Construct** new and healthy cells by providing the body with a strong foundation of water, oxygen, nutritious foods, vitamins, minerals, herbs, cell salts and a lifestyle aimed at keeping the body alkaline.

There is dietary information available online, much of which may only add to your confusion about what is best. Experts contradict each other: some prefer one type of diet or exercise regime over another, or eliminating this over that. But a common message from them all urges us to: eliminate refined sugar, processed foods making up the standard western diet and reduce stress. Increase exercise, eat organic whole foods, sleep more, consume more plants, practice mindfulness and/or meditation.

Think twice before taking the easy route – a pill. A pill does not address the cause; it only treats the symptom. The good news is that the changes necessary to bring about brain health are relatively simple, common sense measures. But simple does not necessarily mean easy, because of the habits and history that got us into the problem in the first instance. As mentioned, detoxification will almost certainly require the guidance of a nutritionist, naturopath or functional medicine professional to ensure decontaminating the body and brain is phased such that the system is upgraded in advance of elimination.

To launch wellbeing from the inside out, we need to address the brain as a processor of information as the brain as an extension of the gut. We can learn to master the challenges. The choice is ours.

# Section 2 Relationships

As Aristotle said, humans are social animals. We establish relationships with others, particularly those who mirror our own lives. We identify ourselves as human beings, but we don't identify with all humans. We divide humans into two categories – those who are like us, and everyone else. Religion, ethnicity, culture, neighbourhoods, clubs, schools and other influences, have a role in shaping the degree of tolerance we have for who and what we are comfortable relating to. But when all is said and done, the basis for all our thoughts, feelings and beliefs boils down to: what is going on inside of me? Herein lies the biggest question of all.

How we engage with others is driven by the programming we experienced as a result of – yes, you guessed - all the forces of family and culture that shaped and groomed, rewarded and punished us until we finally 'got it', and became stuck with it.

But what if we could change being stuck by changing the program? There is no magic wand; the magic lies within each of us. All that is needed is an open mind, new awareness and patience, and the desire for something better.

# 3 Assertiveness

Successful adult relationships are those in which clear, honest communications leads to understanding and mutual respect. In unhealthy relationships, the power-base is often skewed by the absence of these. Assertiveness is the most effective communication style upon which to conduct our relationships. This style allows individuals to act in their own best interests, to stand up for themselves, to express feelings honestly and comfortably and to assert personal rights without denying the rights of others.

Feeling manipulated or dancing to another's tune happens when we are out of our depth, when we experience another's contempt, when we feel unsafe or lack assertiveness. When our sense of self is undermined, we may express our distress outwardly or inwardly as anger, resentment or zoning out, among other states. We are rendered helpless by our impotence, allowing others to bully or manipulate us. Our state is one of not being in control.

The concept of control, then, relates to the power we exercise that determines our potential to influence our actions, others or events.

Dr Julian Rotter, an American psychologist developed the concept of locus of control (LOC) as a way of explaining where our seat of power lies – locus meaning *place*. Either it is within our control or we blame it on some outside influence. **External** LOC means individuals believe their decisions and lives are controlled by factors in their environment, people or circumstances which they cannot influence, or by chance or fate. A typical example of someone with an external LOC might be: 'You *made* me do it!' or 'I'm late because... (fill in the blank)'. In other words, external LOC is about abdicating responsibility or finding an excuse.

Individuals with an **internal** LOC attribute successes or failures to their own actions, reviewing what they did, and either learning the lesson for a better result next time, or acknowledging that the effort they put in paid off, and enjoy the sense of achievement.

A lack of assertiveness is associated with the inability to understand emotions or express them appropriately. I, myself, was someone who lacked that quality in most areas of my life. I was rebellious intermittently, but my 'nice girl/young woman/ daughter/don't-make-waves' persona shone through: compliant, friendly, easygoing – until I'd had enough. When the tipping point came, as it inevitably did, I checked out of the relationship/ course/activity/job. My resentment would grow until something or someone out there had taken advantage of me just once too often; I had been used by 'them' yet again. Take from this that it was always *their* fault.

In my early 20s my tolerance for living at home had reached its limit and I made the decision to live independently. My mother was against the idea. I don't recall having any discussion, devising a plan, or, indeed, giving it much thought. 'Watch me', was the response I can imagine myself typically making as I packed up and left. My lack of awareness and inability to articulate my pent-up frustration forced me beyond my tipping point. One could hardly imagine a less assertive way for an immature young woman to leave home.

This anecdote is offered for no reason other than to illustrate how disempowering a lack of assertiveness can be. Growing up in my family was a good place to be. We were respected and respectable. In my early years my father worked as a travelling salesman, a job that took him away for two weeks, back for a week. I imagine my parents had decided that the discipline and general home and family management, therefore, would fall to my mother. Hers was the way we did things, and it was in that environment that I was shaped.

As a teen I stayed with friends during school holidays, and was amazed to observe how ideas were discussed and developed around the dinner table. I had no reference points for forming or expressing opinions; it just wasn't the way our family communicated. I realised that something was out of sync in my world, but had no idea what to do about it.

## Assertive and Unassertive Behaviour

The absence of assertive awareness left me not knowing what it looked like or how to embrace it. Both my parents lacked assertiveness, but there were many qualities my siblings and I did develop: self-confidence, a social conscience, an understanding of difference, of fairness and justice and support for the underdog. But leaving home in the way I did was an act of hostility. I was unable to express myself any other way.

By contrast, assertive individuals know how to state their opinions and feelings without violating those of others. They have clear boundaries – aware what is theirs and what is not. They recognise and understand their feelings and take responsibility for them. Being assertive is as much about listening as it is about being heard. It is not the opposite of aggression, but something altogether different. The opposite of aggression is passivity, or being a doormat. Assertiveness is about standing up to manipulation, saying 'yes' and 'no' and meaning it. It is about not allowing your strings to be pulled by another. It is about taking one hundred percent responsibility for your part, without excuse.

Seen as the most positive of interpersonal styles, assertiveness is an attitude and skill. It is about listening and questioning to understand. Negotiating or understanding differences rather than being right. It enables the individual to act in their own best interest, stand up for themselves and exercise their rights without denying the rights of others. It provides healthy soil for wellbeing.

## Behaviour Styles

Behaviour is learned. Trapped by habit and/or the lack of an alternative way of communicating, unassertive behaviours, such as aggression, bullying, being passive or passive-aggressive, avoiding, manipulating and accommodating may be used. These are the strategies we developed, sub-consciously, to help us survive in our families and in the world around us.

**Aggression** is the win-lose or lose-lose mentality. It's my way or no way. Aggressive individuals criticise, blame, complain, nag, shout, threaten, punish, bribe or belittle others.

Aggression can be physical, but also can be communicated in non-physical ways. It is behaving in a controlling manner using voice, tone, volume, vocabulary and body language – elements geared to silence or subdue the opponent. Aggression is communicating and behaving with no regard for the feelings, needs or rights of others. It asserts their view with minimal cooperativeness, the goal being to win at all costs, and certainly to have the last word.

The **bully** intimidates or coerces someone to do something at their bidding or face the consequences. This form of aggression can be verbal, emotional, physical and, currently on the rise, cyber. Bullying can be carried out by an individual or a group, and takes place in families, schools, the workplace, in sport and in neighbourhoods – indeed, in any context in which humans interact with each other.

**Passivity**, or allowing oneself to be a doormat, is where the individual denies their own needs in the vain hope of pleasing everyone else. Based on fear and anxiety about experiencing disapproval, upsetting others or feeling unworthy, it correlates with low self-esteem.

'Doormats' take on too much at their own expense. They come from a tradition of giving, giving, giving and then get mad because no one gives back to them. This style, similar to accommodating, is not assertive; its goal is to yield and not to make waves.

Passivity has a legitimate place in situations that require sensitivity, reasonableness, creating goodwill, keeping the peace or for issues of low importance. However, when it is the default response to avoid facing what needs to be faced, it can lead to dissatisfaction and resentment.

**Passive aggressive** behaviour takes many forms, but consists of deliberate, active, but veiled hostile acts. It is where the individual feels angry with someone but does not or cannot tell them. Instead of communicating their upset, annoyance, irritability or disappointment, they instead swallow their feelings, clam up or give angry looks. They may demonstrate their opposition by being sullen and withdrawn, or by exhibiting a negative attitude. They might not always show their anger or resentment, even appearing down-to-earth and polite, friendly, and well-meaning. But beneath the surface the fire is being fuelled. Resentment grows. Passive aggressive behaviour can be covert or overt.

The person who uses **avoidance** satisfies neither their own needs nor those of others. By not engaging, their goal is to stay safe, to avoid risk and confrontation. Avoiders underachieve because they may be fearful of failure, rejection or may simply not be motivated to do the task.

**Manipulators,** those who are indirectly aggressive, use charm, persuasion, coaxing, trickery and misdirection. Their underlying belief is 'I can fool people to get what I want.' Manipulators use agendas known only to themselves, while feigning concern for or interest in the other person.

The exciting thing about behaviour styles is that we have the ability to learn more effective ways of interacting. We weren't born complaining, nagging or undermining others: we adapted to survive our families and other environments with the least amount of pain while maximising reward. If we got approval for being good and not making waves, the pay-off was incentive enough for us to be a goodie-two-shoes, a possible aspect of ourselves we later resent but find difficult to change.

The following wisdom from the Virtues Project ™ struck a chord: 'When we are assertive, we have the strength to resist negative or hurtful influences. We think for ourselves, ask for what we need, and speak up to protect ourselves and others. When we practice assertiveness, we practice self-esteem, citizenship, and valour. Though it may not always seem so, to be assertive is to be a blessing in the world.'[48]

If in doubt about what communication styles you use that are less than acceptable to others, ask a trusted friend. Ask out of curiosity, only if you are open to listening to and taking on board their feedback. These examples show how we can tackle some less-than-effective thoughts and behaviours with more assertive ways.

| Ineffective thought . . . | Assertive . . . |
|---|---|
| I shouldn't say how I'm really feeling or thinking because I don't want to burden others with my problems | I state my thoughts or feelings with clarity, taking full responsibility for my part. I acknowledge myself for being authentic or staying true to my beliefs even though there may be consequences |
| If I assert myself I will upset the other person and ruin our friendship | Say how it is for me with reference to how I am feeling, without blaming the other person or putting them down and demonstrates emotional intelligence |

| Ineffective thought . . . | Assertive . . . |
|---|---|
| It will be terribly embarrassing if I say what I think | Respecting and acknowledging someone else's point of view doesn't mean I accept it, but provides an opportunity to challenge it |
| If someone says 'no' to me it is because they don't like or love me | I asked for a favour. They said 'no', which was their right. They did not reject me, they rejected the request |
| I shouldn't have to say what I need or how I feel: people close to me should already know | No one is a mind-reader. Asking for what I need or saying how I feel is placing my own and others' needs on an equal footing. By doing so I am honouring myself |
| It is uncaring, rude and selfish to say what you want | Acknowledging, expressing and affirming my needs as equal to those of others is not rude or selfish, but honest communication |
| It will all work out in the end, and anyway it's not my fault | By being passive I have no way of influencing the outcome, and I remain a victim |
| People should keep their feelings to themselves | Feelings expressed appropriately can provide feedback for lessons to be learned and allow for richer and deeper relationships |

| Ineffective thought . . . | Assertive . . . |
|---|---|
| If I say that I am feeling anxious or vulnerable people will think I am weak and ridicule me or take advantage of me | People may instead see my struggle and admire me for pushing through and overcoming my challenges. A weakness remains one until I overcome and transform it into a strength |
| If I accept compliments from someone it will mean I am big headed | False modesty is shallow. Genuinely offered compliments acknowledge my contribution. By being authentic, thanking the person and internalising the compliment builds my confidence |

## Assertive Rights

Gael Lindenfield, author and trainer in emotional well-being, provides us with a list of Assertive Rights for the individual, the family and the wider community.[49] Just as the Universal Declaration of Human Rights is a comprehensive statement of the rights to which all human beings are inherently entitled, so, too, are the Assertive Rights – even though not formally enshrined.

1. The right to ask for what we want (realising that the other person has the right to say 'No')
2. The right to have opinions, feelings and emotions and to express them appropriately
3. The right to make statements which may have no logical basis and which we do not have to justify (e.g. intuitive ideas and comments)
4. The right to make our own decisions and to cope with the consequences

5. The right to choose whether or not to get involved in the problems of others

6. The right to know about something but not to understand

7. The right to make mistakes

8. The right to be successful

9. The right to change our mind

10. The right to privacy

11. The right to be alone and independent

12. The right to change ourselves and be assertive people

## Responding to

Rarely are children taught how to respond to criticism, taunts or put-downs. They learn to fly by the seat of their pants; they find a way out of the uncomfortable situation, a pay-off which they will more than likely use again if it worked the first time. As children we might have been confused about what was important – what we were feeling or what we were being asked to do. At time we may have felt discomfort in our bodies, but did not have had the emotional intelligence to understand or articulate what we were experiencing. We learned to duck and dive, deflect or dissolve to temporarily alleviate the pressure. Without the tools to effectively negotiate the interpersonal discomfort of saying 'yes' when we meant 'no', we gave in for the sake of peace, or did not speak up for fear of reprisal. Thus, having missed out on being 'inoculated' against those who were more powerful than our small selves, we fell into habits of being manipulated, humiliated or bullied for the sake of peace or for our own safety.

When a parent brings a child's attention to a task not completed properly, the intention, hopefully, is to use it as a learning point. Sadly, the lesson is often lost because the parent has been critical and used a label such as 'you're lazy' rather than trying to understand why the child had failed. When, 'No, I'm not lazy, you are', is the only response the child can draw from their limited emotional repertoire, they are fighting back by mirroring the insult. (For every push there is an equal and opposite push back.) This typical reaction is the child focussing on the label rather than the emotions she was feeling. Lazy could as easily be substituted with stupid, clumsy or any other label. No surprises here: the label begets defensiveness and the unwanted behaviour goes unchanged; and the opportunity for learning is lost. Any good parent guide would direct its reader to criticise the *behaviour* rather than label the child, but out of ignorance or other pressures, parents and others frequently and unconsciously perpetuate these negative cycles. Under such conditions, the child rarely learns to understand their emotional responses nor effective ways to express themselves.

Behaviour-as-label is the cause of many of our limiting beliefs. We remain stuck in defending a label when our focus should on identifying and naming the feeling. We are not taught and, as adults, did not learn the ways to more effective communication, so remain trapped in the defensive mindset of a seven year-old. Unable to learn assertiveness as children, we continue to use the same impoverished emotional and communications palette into adulthood.

## From Yes to No

Saying 'Yes' or 'No' when we do not mean it can be a difficult habit to break, and is related to item number one in the Assertive Rights charter. Making a choice can be tricky when, in the past, your answer was given to appease someone. Heaven forbid it may suggest that we are selfish, and requires us either to justify why we feel deserving, or to list ten reasons why we've made that choice. Such a habit is very hard to break. The airlines have it right: should the oxygen mask drop from the ceiling, we are instructed to attach ours first before attending to others.

## Assertive Techniques

A key aspect of assertiveness is *how* we respond to requests or criticism – the R in the E + R = O part of the equation over which we have control. How can we step off the treadmill of reactivity? With conscious effort we can learn what our body is telling us, give the feeling a name, discern what is valid and learn new ways.

Valid criticism is something we know to be legitimate, such as on those occasions when we were late or messed up. In those circumstances it is useful to become aware of how our list of excuses compares with taking full responsibility and apologising.

1. **Negative assertion** or **owning up**. Instead of being defensive we can demonstrate our ability to take responsibility and accept the consequences of our behaviour. Saying: 'I'm sorry. Yes, I was late and spoiled Sunday dinner for everyone' or, 'Yes, I agree. I messed up' acknowledges the misdemeanour.
   - Agree with the accusation and acknowledge the mistake. We have all experienced this from the other side and know how much better it makes us feel.
   - Agree with the odds: say something like, 'That's probably true' or 'You're probably right'.
   - Agree in principle: 'We all make mistakes from time to time'

2. **Negative enquiry** is a genuine enquiry, 'What's so bad about me doing . . . ?' or 'What would you like me to have done instead?'

3. **Broken record** (and if you're young you may not know what this means) is simply repeating your request or refusal, such as 'I want my money back'. Expressed firmly, consistently and resolutely without justification or explanation, it may require an increase in volume, tone or pace while remaining calm. After three or four repeats of the same phrase, you can respond with silence. The key is to maintain respect for the other person while standing firm with your simple message.

4. **Buying time** gives you time to consider a request. Your response could be something like, 'Can I get back to you on that?' or 'I'll need time to consider your request – I'll get back to you today/ tomorrow/next week'. Another gracious response would be: 'If you need an answer now, it's NO. If you give me time to consider, I'll get back to you by ...' This removes the pressure and covers your bases.

5. **I-statements** indicate you are taking responsibility for what's going on. An easy four-step method can bring about fresh results:

Step 1. Use 'I', not 'you'

Step 2. Refer to the **behaviour** *not* to the person

    (in other words, drop the label)

Step 3. State how the behaviour affects you

Step 4. State what you need to happen

So instead of, 'You make me so angry when you're late!', try

> 'I felt **anxious** when you **arrived home at 3:30 instead of 2:00** because I **thought something might have happened.** In future I would like **you to text or phone that you'll be late.**'

46

6. **Self-disclosure** explains what you are feeling and helps others understand why you are doing what you are doing. Once again it demonstrates that you are taking full responsibility for your side of the transaction. 'I feel awkward saying no to your request for a loan' or, 'I'm uncomfortable asking you to babysit again and I know it's short notice, but I'm in a tight corner for this evening'.

7. The **'NO' Sandwich** is similar to self-disclosure in a simple three-step process. It will come easily and naturally with practice, and will change your life:

   Step 1 Acknowledge the request / validate the point

   Step 2 Refuse with something like, 'Sorry, not this time' without giving reasons

   Step 3 Next step – wrap up courteously

   – Acknowledge the request: 'I know it's late and you don't want to wait for the bus.'

   – Refuse 'I'm sorry I can't drop you home.'

   – Next step 'Any other time I would love to have helped you out, but unfortunately I cannot do it this evening.'

   No excuses. No justification. No explanation.

   Your friend may persist in the hope that you will take responsibility for their problem. Your job is to mix and match your portfolio of responses: become the broken record or use self-disclosure in answer to their request until they give up. If they get angry, it is their attempt to manipulate you into feeling guilty and giving in. Remember, you are refusing the request, not the person. And don't forget to remind yourself that it is not your problem. When you distance yourself from the habit of feeling guilty or selfish, you avoid the trap of being the solution. By standing up for yourself you have honoured your own needs – and are no longer a doormat.

8. **Invalid criticism** is when we are accused of something that is untrue. Perhaps you were accused of being 'mean', when you know you were not. Invalid criticism is unfair and designed to put you down or undermine you. If it does not belong to you, you do not need to defend it. You make a statement like, 'That's completely untrue! On the contrary,..' Without being defensive or expressing anger, your response is delivered with conviction, in an even but firm tone of voice that matches your body language; unambiguous and authoritative.

The joy of assertiveness is that we can learn and practice it until we become . . . assertive. We have practiced pausing before we respond rather than defaulting to old habits. We are learning, building confidence, taking responsibility and nurturing ourselves to stand tall and take pride in our growth.

An important clue is this: how we feel in our bodies can help us to become aware that something is amiss. It is time to stop ignoring the spasm, butterflies, clenched fist or headache and instead check in with yourself about what's going on. Rather than *dismiss the feeling*, learn to understand what *message* it is giving you. Honour and trust its authenticity. Name it. Regard it as an ally with valuable information that something is out of kilter. **Every** message your body gives you is an opportunity for learning and growth. The bad news, tragically, is that opportunities lost, are lost. The good news is that there will always be others. Our choice is to reap the benefits or lose the learning. The more we practice assertiveness, the more resilient our internal locus of control and sense of wellbeing will be.

– Start by practicing one method.

- Try it out in your head.
- Try it out loud with yourself.
- Then try it out in real time in a real situation.
- Review how it went and how it felt.
- Think through how it could be better next time if it didn't go quite as well as you had hoped.

Feel the pleasure of that shifting power base as you learn the empowering art of assertiveness.

# 4 Personal Boundaries

Whichever way we look at them, personal boundaries are like property boundaries. They are there to protect our interests. We recognise property demarcation by a hedge or a fence. We may even understand that a grass verge alone, with no barrier present, indicates a boundary line.

A boundary, then, can be a solid thing like a wall, or a few posts spaced on the ground. Some are impregnable, some breachable. However, all are markers which draw a line separating where one ownership ends and another begins. They define what belongs to us and what does not. By law, for example, you are entitled to cut the overhang from your neighbour's tree which crosses the boundary line and return the cuttings to their yard. It is theirs, not yours. You are free to return them by right. Assertiveness is an essential skill in the battle to set and retain personal boundaries. Boundaries are knowing where the line is; assertiveness communicates to others where it is. When we are clear with ourselves and others and use all our resources to identify and protect our boundaries, we enjoy the benefits of wellbeing.

## The Importance of Boundaries

Personal boundaries fall into two categories: emotional and physical. They are robust when the individual takes responsibility for their own actions and emotions. People with strong boundaries are confident, have good levels of self-esteem and communicate their message clearly and unambiguously. In fact, boundary strength can be regarded as a measure of an individual's sense of self-worth – strong or weak, there's a correlation with how they feel about themselves.

The absence of boundaries and the absence of the power to defend them can lead us to lives that are fear-based, not believing that we are entitled to protect ourselves from the self-serving intentions of others.

People with poor boundaries typically take too much responsibility for the emotions or actions of others, or may expect others to take responsibility for theirs. The absence of responsibility inevitably backfires, leaving the individual with a compromised sense of their own identity and low self-esteem. They find themselves:

- being taken advantage of
- helping people out even when it's not convenient, and then feeling resentful
- feeling controlled
- being caught up in dramas not of their own making, yet feeling unable to extricate themselves
- being defensive
- placing greater value on the opinions of others than on their own

Resilient boundaries provide clarity about what belongs to me, and what does not. A strong boundary keeps the good in and the bad out. Unclear or weak boundaries can lead to interpretations that serve one party more than another, leaving one triumphant, the other frustrated, feeling encroached upon or violated.

Personal boundaries are crucial in helping us enjoy healthy relationships and situations and avoiding unhealthy or dysfunctional ones. Boundaries set parameters that define emotional and personal space and are important for people of all ages to understand.

All boundary violations as a form of control use manipulation, anger, coercion, threat, harassment, intimidation and other pressures by one party over another.

Physical boundaries, sometimes called *personal space,* is a concept with which many are familiar. Who hasn't queued in the bank or supermarket where the person behind you stands too close for comfort? You inch forward and they follow, oblivious to your disquiet. Equally unsettling may be a hug or other physical contact, a joke or language use that triggers an unpleasant gut reaction. In each instance our personal boundary has been violated.

Personal space varies from individual to individual, and within the individual at different times. It is set by the individual, rather than imposed from the outside. A loved one's proximity after a row might feel too close, or may be experienced as too distant if the mood is joyful and loving or if we need reassurance or comfort.

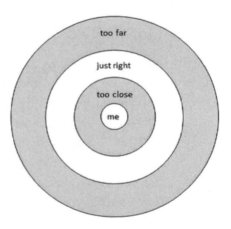

**Model of Personal Space Boundaries**

When a boundary violation is experienced, be warned: it's not the other person's behaviour or intention that matters – they may think a touch is a sign of affection – it's the effect the gesture has on the receiver. Trust it and act accordingly.

Individuals with leaky boundaries tolerate transgressions in social situations, at work, in the playground and on the Internet, to their cost. All forms of abuse are boundary violations and all boundary violations are forms of abuse.

Sexual abuse, rape, physical abuse and murder are boundary violations at the top end of the scale.

## Boundaries and social media

Don't ever be fooled into believing that ALL behaviour is rational and voluntary. It is frequently adaptive, configuring itself to the demands of the situation. Today the phenomena of social media and Internet chatrooms require, more than ever, that young and old (and everyone in between) understand the necessity for setting boundaries: limits to what the individual will and will not accept and what they will and will not disclose. In other words, everyone needs to be savvy, alert to potential exploitation and confident of where and when to draw a line. Innocence online in the manipulators hands are ingredients for the perfect storm. Individuals need to be clear, and not necessarily polite, to avoid being manipulated or ensnared in the designs of others. Risks to people of all ages – like cyberbullying, being forced to divulge personal and financial information, being befriended or groomed by unknown people – are all disasters waiting to happen.

Sometimes we find ourselves in a double bind – dilemmas requiring equally unpalatable responses whichever option we choose, and from which there appears to be no escape or opt-out clause. We sense someone is taking advantage of us, but were raised to believe that being polite was more important than being clear about where to draw the line. Or perhaps communication couched in flattery or empty promises is more difficult to back away from once a chat room 'relationship' has been established. When our emotions have been engaged: the difficulty of saying 'NO' will often leave us vulnerable to the malevolent intentions of others.

Channel 4's documentary *Hunting the Paedophiles: Inside The National Crime Agency* (2015),[50] exposed different levels of blackmail of 18,000 plus young boys, the majority of whom lived in the UK, who were cajoled into extreme behaviour. The lure of a seductive 15-year old girl as a front soon escalated into depravity. The boys became victims because they did not know how to say 'no' to the beautiful girl. The perverts lured the boys into sexually compromising situations, subsequently leveraging the situation to encourage the boys into still greater acts of indecency by threatening them with exposure on social media, to their parents and schools – the perfect double bind. When eventually traced and arrested, the reason the perverts gave for targeting English boys was that, unlike their USA and European counterparts, they found it difficult to say 'no'.

The risk to Irish children of cyberbullying, grooming and exploitation has been variously reported in The Irish Times, The Examiner and other media as being between 25% and 33%. The EU has created annual Safer Internet Day (is one day in the year enough?), yet headlines proclaim that online child grooming is an 'ongoing struggle'. Setting personal boundaries is not some airy-fairy concept: alerting everyone to the need for healthy boundaries should be a local and international imperative.

Appropriate education and awareness has the potential to enable all of us to recognise and resist abuse, victimisation, bullying or, indeed, any upsetting, unsafe, threatening or dangerous situations.The Stay Safe programme in Ireland reaches primary school children, but should not stop once they achieve the age of twelve. Everyone, from children through to the elderly, is a potential victim because so many of us have been groomed by our culture, like the 18,000 English boys, to be *nice*.

Emotions direct our behaviour, and are a complex tangle of our cognitive and perceptual processes. Exploitative grooming for financial or sexual gain works methodically to build trust and to lure the victim into feeling special. It can happen to anyone. A groomer striking too early will spook the victim, so they bide their time, offering friendship and promises. Once the victim's guard is down, the perpetrator will do something for the victim so that they will feel *indebted*. The groomer will endeavour to ensure their 'special relationship' is kept secret. Unaware of the groomer's true intention, the victim will often instinctively feel that something is not right. But because of the allure and excitement, the victim may ignore these small alarm bells until it seems too late. But it's never too late. Even in the face of threats, the victim should immediately cease the contact, recognising that the groomer has used manipulation for personal gain. The victim owes him nothing, and certainly not politeness.[51]

In an attempt to prevent abuse from occurring and to educate young people and others to build the capacity to pre-empt abuse, family and community conversations could follow some of these guidelines:

- Ensure the victim knows it's not their fault, even if they feel they've done something silly.
- Save any evidence and show it to someone who can help or who is in authority.
- Tell the aggressor to stop or cease all communications immediately.
- It's alright to ask for help.
- Use available tech tools to block the aggressor.
- Protect accounts by not sharing passwords with anyone – your friend today may not be tomorrow.

   — If you suspect or know someone is being bullied, take action.

In relation to grooming young people, and without oversimplifying this very complex issue, two questions requiring black and white answers (no grey allowed) might be:

1.  Can I be absolutely certain that the person with whom I am interacting online is actually who they say they are?
2.  What would I feel if my . . . (mother/father/daughter/son/employer/community) found out about this?

If there is even a hint of uncertainty amidst the excitement, then contact should be severed immediately.

## Everyday manipulation and boundaries

Exhibiting strong boundaries and being assertive are synonymous. On the lower end of the violations continuum, an innocuous everyday event that exemplifies leaky boundaries between siblings could be a conversation such as:

| | |
|---|---|
| Marcella | Hi Sis, how're things? |
| Jane | Great thanks. How're you and the kids? |
| Marcella | Well, that's just what I wanted to talk to you about. I have an appointment tomorrow evening at 7.00. Can you babysit for a couple of hours? |
| Jane | Tomorrow evening? No sorry, Marcie, I've got plans of my own. |
| Marcella | Why? What are you doing? |
| Jane | Well, you know my friend Grainne? I'm going over to chat about her 21st. |

| | |
|---|---|
| Marcella | Sure, you can do that any time. Just ring her and tell her something urgent has come up. She'll understand. |
| Jane | It's her 21st in a fortnight. She wants to finalise her invitations. |
| Marcella | She can do that without you or you can meet up another time. I really need you to babysit. Just for a couple of hours . . . . |
| Jane | You always do this to me. Last minute. It makes me mad. |
| Marcella | Well, I've got my hands full with the kids and Martin, not to mention the damn dog. All you do is look after yourself. All I'm asking is a small favour. |
| Jane | It's not fair. I dunno . . . |
| Marcella | Karen and Séamus are looking forward to seeing you — they really like it when you babysit. They haven't seen you in weeks. |
| Jane | I'd really prefer not to . . . |
| Marcella | Now you're being selfish. Just give us a dig out with the kids, will you! Grainne will understand. |

Jane's lack of awareness of whose problem it is has allowed Marcella to drive her own agenda through the permeable boundary Jane was trying desperately to hold. Marcella had a problem and looked to Jane for a quick and easy solution. When Jane resisted, Marcella immediately switched to emotional exploitation that made Jane the problem. Accused of selfishness and feeling guilty, Jane succumbed to pressure and became a victim.

As soon as we give up our resolve and slip into becoming the solution to the other person's problem, we have lost our line of defence – our boundary. Fortunately, when this happens we experience the intrusion in our physiology, that feeling in our throat or gut. The body has the wisdom to know where the limit is, even if the head does not.

A person with clear personal boundaries:

- is assertive
- has a strong sense of self
- says yes or no without feelings of guilt or being beholden to anyone
- does not feel the need to justify their decisions
- is balanced
- responds from a position of being firmly grounded in the present (does not refer to the past or the future)
- does not put themselves or others down

In this checklist there is no hint of selfishness or being driven by a defensive, manipulative or acquisitive agenda. It is simple and clear. When we learn to interpret our gut feelings as an ally, we are on the way to being able to make decisions based on a different, self-protective rationale. We assert our right to express our feelings and opinions, to be treated with respect, to set our own priorities and to say no without feeling guilty. We make the decision to babysit or not based on weighing up our priorities. We are no longer victims to manipulation by others, nor are we the answer to their problem.

With the above in mind, a 'holding onto her boundary' conversation by Jane might otherwise have gone something like:

| | |
|---|---|
| Jane | Well, you know my friend Grainne? I'm going over to chat about her 21st. |
| Marcella | Sure, you can do that any time. Just ring her and tell her something urgent has come up. She'll understand. |
| Jane | It's an arrangement I've made that I don't want to change. |
| Marcella | She can do that without you or you can meet up with her another time. I really need you to babysit. Just for a couple of hours . . . . |
| Jane | Sorry Marcie. I'm sticking with my arrangement. Maybe another time. |
| Marcella | Well, I've got my hands full with the kids and Martin, not to mention the damn dog. All you do is look after yourself. She'll understand if you change the arrangements. |
| Jane | She might understand, but I don't want to. Sorry Marcie – any other evening but not tomorrow. (And use as many of the assertive techniques outlined in the previous chapter as necessary, like the broken record or the 'no'sandwich). |

Unlike in the first scenario, this conversation ensures Jane's personal boundary remains intact. By refusing to take ownership of Marcella's problem, she is able to avoid the manipulative trap - her 'job' is to ensure it remains Marcella's problem. Jane is saying no to the problem. She has recognised her sister's manipulative tack and decided that, on this occasion, she will not be coerced. Her new, more empowered strategy has given her permission to consider the options, decide what she wants and then express this clearly.

Had Marcella used a different approach, taken responsibility for her request, recognised Jane's arrangement had equal validity, and appealed instead to Jane's goodwill rather than impose guilt or shame, the outcome might have been different. The difference between the two approaches lies in the intention of the person making the request. When a boundary is breached, we have the right to say no.

If a tactic like this resonates with you, pause. Learn to question the intention behind requests and check in with yourself about what you really want to do. Be firm in claiming and owning your own power. It gets easier with practice and is something we can all learn.

Pause and take note: who are the people who encourage your growth, and who stifles it? As with habits, we need to review our support team among family and friends. We can lovingly distance or detach from others in order to care for ourselves, and nurture relationships that bring love, growth and healing. Melanie Beattie, author of *Codependent No More*, asserts that each of us has a primary responsibility in life to detach from obsessions, habits and people that do not serve our best interests.[52]

Let's learn to recognise the moment our instinct sends us a warning signal. Let's begin to engage our executive brain and pause before reacting. Consider your needs, decide on what course of action to take, and then move in that new direction. Move forward without defaulting to the outdated responses you have been trapped up to now. Engage fully with the process. Decide on what you need before the next time, because once you are clear where to draw the line ahead of the next request it is easier to plot your course. Decide on *your* rules. Trust your gut. Set your parameters. Practice. Enjoy the results. And practice some more.

# 5 Communicating and Influencing

We communicate publicly and privately, consciously and unconsciously. It is all learned, second nature behaviour. Communication uses multiple channels of tone, pitch, volume, body language and vocabulary, among others. Why do we communicate? To convey information, share knowledge, to persuade, to lure, to flatter, to build understanding, express feelings or to tell someone to get lost. This chapter looks at several aspects of communication and how different styles can help or hinder us on our path to wellbeing.

Communication can be formal, informal, friendly, hostile or plain boring. We can say something without words. We can say something and mean something completely different. We can break the rules and get away with it, or we can break the rules and . . . not get the job, have our proposal rejected, or simply fail to get the message across. Communication can involve others, or can be something that goes on inside our heads – what we should have said or will say next time. Even in our dreams we 'see' images and experience emotion – forms of communication. There are probably very few minutes, if any, in every twenty-four hour cycle that we are not actually communicating, either with ourselves or others.

As social beings, the relationships that matter are those that give us something and those to which we contribute in return. We all know someone who talks and talks with hardly a breath but who actually says very little, or someone who is sometimes inappropriate or silent or overbearing. Healthy communication is where there is give and take, where there is balance and meaning between and among participants.

In my family of origin we communicated politely; never screamed or shouted at each other. Our behaviour as children could be controlled by a look, or the threat of being put out of the car with bus fare home. As siblings we didn't negotiate, we fought and either won or gave up. If we swore, we suffered soap in the mouth. My mother made sure things were orderly and done the right way. I have no memory of learning how to play with alternative viewpoints. Things were simply the way they were.

I recall being asked as a teen by a friend of the family what film I would like to go and see. When I replied, 'I don't mind', he rounded on me: 'You should mind. You should have an idea or opinion on EVERYTHING.' Perhaps it was his insistence that I 'should', but in an instant I dismissed his advice on having a personal opinion or exercising choice – after all, he was 'old', had a drink problem and was a wannabe writer whom I knew with absolute certainty would never complete a manuscript. His only influence was to reaffirm my belief that I did not have to have an opinion. Whatever didn't fit into my model of the world was simply rejected.

It was years later that his advice came back to haunt me. I came to see my communication style as not very influential. If I bent whichever way the wind blew or was carried by whatever current was the strongest, I would end up somewhere I had not chosen to be. There had to be a different way.

Learning to make fresh and sometimes scary choices was new territory. I had never been through the hammering and smelting process needed to untangle my thoughts or feelings. My filters were black or white: this was acceptable, that was not. I accepted or rejected everything at face value, never asking *why*. Utterly naive, I was unaware of how to look behind my automatic responses to grasp what others were saying. I lacked curiosity about their thoughts or opinions, accepting or rejecting them instantaneously because I already knew what I knew.

## Communication as an exchange

The distance travelled since then has given me greater discernment about what to express, how to express it, and to whom. I learned to remove the black and white filter and replace it with one of curiosity, active listening, and the ability to ask for more information. My way of disengaging was upgraded to what else?, why?, what if?. I had finally come to appreciate the value of two-way communication.

Stephen Covey provides us with a credible metaphor of communication as an exchange – the Emotional Bank Account (EBA).[53] The EBA represents the value invested in our relationships, influenced by the numerous ways in which we choose to share information. If we have a healthy balance in our EBA there is a high level of trust and enough in reserve to compensate for a withdrawal. When our bank balance is low or overdrawn, resentments cloud exchanges. As any bank manager knows, overdrawn accounts are bad news.

Psychologists who have studied and measured the ratio of deposits to withdrawals, declare that the optimal score is 5:1.[54] That is five gives to every one take. This ratio is significant for a relationship to flourish, meaning for every burst of irritability, every tense exchange, every negative thought and expression of disappointment, there have to be not double, but five times as many deposits. Making an emotional deposit can be as simple as apologising for an omission, expressing thanks or making a cup of tea without being asked. A withdrawal might be accepting that same cup of tea without a nod of acknowledgement, expecting dinner not to be dried out, even though you didn't phone to say you'd be two hours late, or being angry for being called on to discipline the children in the middle of your team's cup final on TV. It is the frequent small positive interactions that tip the goodwill scales, not the one-off statements like a rip-roaring birthday bash.

An average of 3:1, three positives to one negative, achieves the minimum to stay well and manage an ordinary life. A ratio falling below 3:1, and staying down, is the slippery slope from which it is hard to recover.

If the deposits creep beyond five, the balance tips the other way: the depositer can soon feel undervalued for being the one who gives, gives, gives. A consistent ratio of 11:1 positive to negative signals an imbalance and hides the real problem. Appropriate communication – particularly when addressing difficulties or unacceptable behaviour – has an important role to play in creating the sound foundation necessary for relationships to flourish. Where imbalance becomes chronic and the ratio deviates from 5:1, up or down the scale, the hastier the demise of the relationship.

## Self-talk

Because communication is something we engage in with ourselves, we need to be mindful of what we are saying to ourselves inside our heads. When we feel anger, guilt or shame, what are we telling ourselves? The reality of communications is that, whether it is with someone else or a conversation going on internally, the messages and images we receive reverberate in our emotional brain centre, bouncing off walls layered with years of repetition. It's me putting myself down. These self-inflicted dispatches also require the attention and generosity of the 5:1 ratio. If I put myself down once, I need to give myself five positives. Anything less maintains the status quo of my depleted sense of self – low self-esteem.

Hebb's Law states that neurons that fire together wire together,[55] meaning that something repeated often enough ensures it stays in our memory bank. Now whether we do it to ourselves or it is done by others, the power of repeated messages increases their meaning. Our general practice is to put ourselves down more often than we raise ourselves up. The question is: why? Hundreds of studies provide the answer – the power of negative over positive exists in the form 'bad is stronger than good.'[56] How can this be?

In evolutionary terms, negative reactions were the brain's threat (or perceived threat) signal to survival. There was no threat in comfort. The trouble was if you missed a threat you would not be around to enjoy the next pleasurable moment. Being primed for 'bad' or threat was a greater predictor of survival, while reaction to positives was less critical. In order to counteract this imbalance, becoming aware of, and then taking action to fire and wire positive self-talk is a crucial step in the process of building ourselves up from the inside out. Press the pause button before reacting, R, in the E+R=O sequence, take stock, give yourself the opportunity to make a different choice: different choice equals different outcome.

Positive emotion, engagement and positive relationships are pre-requisites for wellbeing.[57] When we are in a good place, clear about who we are and with established boundaries, our effectiveness, relationships and influence will be more functional and productive.

## Communicating non-verbally

Congruence, or its lack between words and the message conveyed, is signalled through non-verbal communication or body language. Would you believe someone whose head was down, shoulders slumped with a deadpan expression saying they felt on top of the world? A formula proposed by a psychologist called Mehrabian in the 1960s observed and analysed the physical expression of communication, where he apportioned fifty-five percent to body language, thirty-eight percent to tone of voice, and only seven percent to the actual words. His 55/38/7 percentage breakdown has been disputed, but the point is that we read posture, facial expression, gesture, eye movement, pace, touch and the use of space to give credence to words. We draw conclusions on the veracity of what has been said by how congruent words are with the body's message, body language always imparting greater meaning than words.

In my work as a coach, I would often ask a client to notice their posture when talking about disappointment, anger or other negative emotion. When asked to visualise themselves feeling proud, strong and powerful, they automatically adjust their posture by straightening up, putting their shoulders back, lifting the chin. I have them close their eyes to really occupy the revised posture, feel the shape, locate their core, where in the body they feel their strength. Feeling depressed or upbeat, it doesn't matter which, is mirrored by the body. There has to be congruence for it to feel real.

Congruence is how a gifted actor conveys true character in diverse roles. Total immersion with the character is how we perceive them as credible. Not everything is as simple as change-the-posture, change-the-experience, but it is nevertheless how we place our faith in others. Who would vote for a potential candidate whose body posture and energy levels were suspect? We can and do influence others by appearing confident – and the spin-off is that we can begin to believe it of ourselves – a thumbs-up posture automatically generates thumbs-up neurotransmitters, setting up a physiological cycle of success.

The 'fake it 'til you make it' cliché is supported by research: the influence of posture alone meant that people who maintained a power pose versus a meek pose showed a decrease in stress hormones and an increase in hormones related to dominance and confidence.[58] One conclusion is that our posture influences how we think and feel; change our posture, change how we feel. Posture conveys emotion. In fact, brain research shows that whatever we are feeling starts in the body, and only later (nanoseconds later) in the conscious mind. So, if we're hungry, or impatient, or angry, or happy, the body reliably signals the feeling and delivers the relevant hormones *before* our conscious mind gets the message.[59]

Thanks to evolution, the much faster unconscious mind was selected to handle the job of survival. It ensured optimal fight, flight or freeze reactions rather than risk crucial decisions with the slower conscious mind. Deliberately and consciously smiling, laughing or feeling confident, or even pretending to, sets off biological processes that alter our body's chemistry epigenetically.[60] (There is more on this in chapter 13). The happy neurotransmitters provide a DIY antidote to shift our mood and put us in an improved state of mind.

Perhaps it is time to create and practice new ways of communicating. Tragically, many of us spend more time planning our holiday than planning our lives. Decide on what it is you want. Rehearse it. Become it in practice, just as an actor takes on the authenticity of a role. Adjust your posture to mirror what you aspire to, long before you believe it. Be the main actor in your story. Use your body's wisdom to shape the direction of how you want to show up. Be the hero. Use whole-brain thinking to make breakthroughs. Think outside the box. Start communicating with yourself and others deliberately and boldly. Be courageous - create a brave new world for yours.

# 6 Anger and Trauma

Anger and trauma are different, in that anger is a primary feeling or emotion, while trauma results from an unexpected or distressing event. Anger is often a large part of a survivor's response to trauma. While anger may help us cope with life's stresses, it can also create problems in the lives of those who have experienced trauma. Instead of regarding the universal emotion of anger as one of life's torments, it would benefit us to see it instead as an ally. This chapter looks at anger and trauma separately and jointly.

## Anger – friend or foe?

Anger is similar to a yellow card received by a soccer player for the infraction of a rule – it brings attention to a violation. In our life and in our environments, when a social norm or rule is broken or something goes wrong, we experience it viscerally, feeling it, perhaps, in the pit of the stomach, jaw or fist. It feels like an assault of some kind. Anger prepares us for fight, flight or freeze through changes in our physiology: our heart rate increases, our breathing quickens, hormones are released. Anger lets us know that something is wrong, that a line has been crossed; it has primed the body for action.

Many emotions resolve spontaneously – but anger is rarely one of those. Rather, it serves a purpose: once we understand that anger is alerting us to something that is bothering us, we can more easily understand what lies behind the upset and learn from it. Anger frequently is a reaction to feeling afraid, or sad, disappointed, hurt, defiant, being taken for granted or numerous other experiences. In other words anger, a primal survival mechanism, may mask some other emotion.

Harriet Lerner,[61] in her book *The Dance of Anger,* recommends that when we peel back the feeling of anger or rage to understand the underlying issue, we almost certainly will discover some other state of mind such as did we feel humiliated? Not listened to? Undermined? Devastated? Overruled? Bullied?

Once we discover the feeling that was being camouflaged, we can better understand our complex emotional landscapes. Understanding the why and what of our anger opens the door to understanding ourselves with compassion; we are better placed to react less and to express our feelings constructively.

Lower down the 'anger scale' are the less intense feelings of annoyance, displeasure, hostility or irritation that could escalate into rage if left unchecked. It all depends on the extent of the violation, the circumstances and the individual's emotional state at the time.

Anger is relative. If you were bumped as you were approaching the stadium for a U2 concert, you'd hardly notice it. You might feel irritated if someone bumped into you on the street and continued on their way without so much as an apology. However, should a friend bump into you and not apologise, your level of irritation may demand an apology. In other words, the degree to which we react varies depending on how we are feeling, who bumps whom, how they react, the context, and a host of other variables.

If we hold on to anger and stew in it, we turn small events into big ones. Our storehouse of anger accumulates each time we compromise, swallow our words or trade our needs for third party approval. In this way it is not only others who devalue our emotions – we are experts at undermining our feelings ourselves.

Appropriately expressed anger is a positive life force. In his book *The Anger Solution,* John Lee likens it to a spring where water flows up and out, released into the world. When blocked, that same energy remains in the body, generates stress, stagnates, becomes toxic or explodes out. Instead of replaying the scenario again and again, a potential growth point is to check in with yourself and review what happened to cause the emotion. What was the violation and what is the feeling being hidden by the anger? Name it, acknowledge what's truly going on, and learn to express it appropriately.

If we are taken over by the downstairs survival brain and explode in anger or rage, we may be dismissed as unreasonable or troublesome. This can deprive us of the opportunity to have our message heard and thus experience a double put-down: not only have we lost our audience, but we punish ourselves by replaying the scene over and over.

As children, many of us may have been punished for an outburst of anger. Our parents may have lacked the understanding necessary to help us work through and resolve our emotions, not because they were deliberately negligent, but because they did not know how to do it for themselves. The sad part about our early years is that many of us were not taught to understand our feelings, and then grew through our teens and into adults still in the dark.

Out of ignorance we have lurched between left and right brains, or remained entrenched in the downstairs, reactive brain. We are constantly reminded of our hurts and betrayals, but have no alternative to draw on. So instead we deflect our anger by opting out or using sarcasm, shame, blame, disdain or put-downs which yield no (or perhaps a brief) sense of satisfaction. We often feel regret after inappropriately expressing our anger, then continue to replay the incident long after it has passed. Our systems continue to be flooded with toxins, accumulating and reinforcing the belief that *nobody cares what I'm feeling* or *this is just the way I am* or, ... or, ... or.

Anger understood and appropriately expressed is constructive. The inappropriate expression of it reminds us of its ugly face. Most childish outbursts are punished in some way, perhaps by being grounded, ignored, slapped, silenced or given any number of other treatments. The lesson learned early was that it was not acceptable to express anger. This soon led us into habits of repression or avoidance. The threat of punishment shaped our learning. Infringements incurred penalties, so we learned to avoid them.

Anger can be experienced by individuals, families, communities, sports teams, ethnic groups, groups of workers, nations – wherever a perceived or real injustice occurs. What did Nelson Mandela, Lech Walesa or Rosa Parks do to allow their anger to flow and be released, and thus bring about transformation? It would pay to learn how they managed their experience of injustice to bring about such significant and far-reaching personal and political change.

## Rules

Wherever we have people, we have rules. It is the system that shapes 'how things should be' and enables the wheels to turn. We even have systems in place to ensure, as far as possible, that citizens abide by the rules, or face the consequences if they do not.

There are rules for just about every aspect of living - those that are external and imposed from the outside. Then we have those we have signed up to on the inside; a self-imposed internal structure of beliefs and values, called personal rules, which can be self-supportive or oppressive.

What we regard as the rules can be legal and enforceable, or imposed by the culture, religion, gender or our own life experience; those that begin with *you shouldn't* . . . or *boys don't* . . . Then there are the 'can' and 'must' directives, the 'dos' and 'don'ts', all of which carry some consequence – even if self-inflicted. To park on double yellow lines is illegal. We know the rule, yet weigh up the chances because we're going to leave the car for less than a minute. There is a penalty, but only if we're caught.

Some rules we are aware of, others we've taken on board without conscious consideration. Personal rules are the commandments by which we conduct our lives. They may serve us, like showing courtesy by always saying thank you, or they may not. An example of a personal rule that guides our living might be: I never text from my phone when in the company of another person. This private rule that you alone know about nevertheless governs your behaviour. When you are in the company of another and they start texting from their phone, you feel a sense of violation: after all, you respect their presence, why don't they respect yours? But, of course, their sense of right or wrong may differ from yours. Rules, and as a direct result your response, can be logical or illogical.

## Trauma

Traumatic or disturbing events that infringe our boundaries or threaten our sense of control may reduce our capacity to integrate a situation. If not integrated, the event may become lodged as a blockage and can affect the victim emotionally, physiologically, mentally or psychologically. Qualifying events (listed in the handbook used by health care professionals around the world as the authoritative guide to the diagnosis of mental disorders)[62] are often referred to as 'Big T' trauma. What comes to mind is threatened or actual injury, cataclysmic events, war, death or sexual assault. Trauma may be direct, indirect or witnessed by us, or may have been something experienced by someone who is close to us.

Trauma from minor events is more common and known as 'Small t' trauma. Both Big T and Small t trauma leave behind an **energy im-**

**print**, a memory of the trauma that is lodged in the body, affecting organs, tissue and brain.[63]

When the survival instinct of fight, flee or freeze occurs, trauma may occur. Trauma specialist Dr Robert Scaer regards the occasions when trauma is NOT discharged through fight or flight as locking that event into a 'trauma capsule'. In the animal world when an animal freezes and survives, it goes through a period of discharging the high levels of arousal through trembling, running movements, shaking and deep breathing, after which the animal returns to its prior state of calm alertness.[64] In people, when the trauma reaction is not discharged, a belief or unconscious pattern of behaviour is created in that moment. In other words, trauma is lodged in the body as a memory at a molecular level. It is this linking of events that is the body-mind connection.

Not everyone experiencing a catastrophic event will be traumatised to the same degree. One example that comes to mind is soldiers returning from war: some develop PTSD (Post Traumatic Stress Disorder) while others do not. It is not the trauma of war, itself, that creates the problem, but rather the undischarged belief formed or conclusion drawn as a result of the experience that persists and influences the individual's future thoughts and decisions. Through Scaer's work there is strong evidence that traumatic experiences are cumulative, producing heightened arousal with additional unresolved trauma.

Possibly less easy to grasp, but something that affects everyone, is Small t trauma, described as insignificant or passing everyday events. Let's say Mary was drawing with her new markers, lost in her little world of creating a beautiful picture for her mummy. Her mother enters the room and sees marker stains all over a precious table cloth. She yells at or punishes Mary. Mary's world crashes around her; she is in shock. Mary as an adult, having forgotten this particular incident, may nevertheless be filled with self-doubt about how her gesture will be received when doing something nice for someone or giving them a gift.

According to Meta-Medicine – health awareness via the mind-body connection – both Big T and Small t trauma occur in an 'Unexpected, **D**ramatic, **I**solating for which there is **N**o Strategy' (UDIN) moment. It is as if our brains absorb and retain the sounds, sights, smells, taste and touch of everything in that moment. Why? Because recording the event as a potential threat is part of our survival mechanism:[65] UDIN moments are 'perfect storm' conditions that conspire when:

- something happens for which we are unprepared; it occurs **U**nexpectedly
- the event or circumstance is sudden and striking, and therefore **D**ramatic
- we lack the resources to cope, feel alone or apart from others and therefore **I**solated
- we feel a sense of helplessness, with **N**o Strategy on which to rely

However illogical, a UDIN moment, causing the subconscious to make sense of the event, gives it meaning. A simple example might be the loss of a pet.

| Event | Condition | Response |
|-------|-----------|----------|
| Pete's cat is run over. He'd had it since it was a kitten | **U**nexpected | When he went to school he had a cat. When he came home his cat was dead. |
| | **D**ramatic | He was shocked and sad and cried a lot. |
| | **I**solation | Pete's mother explained that it had been an accident and that the cat had not suffered. He should stop crying, and that they could get another cat - another black and white one if he wanted. |
| | **N**o strategy | Pete didn't want another cat. No cat could replace Mittens. His mother didn't understand how much he had loved Mittens |

The meaning Pete might assign to this event could have been:

**Distorted belief 1:** His feelings do not count, or perhaps

**Distorted belief 2:** Generalised to never owning another cat because he did not want to re-experience the pain.

As already mentioned, reactions which are not expressed, experienced, resolved and integrated become blocked and locked as personal baggage. The risk is that, being unaware of how the belief or feeling was formed, we remain helpless and understand that 'this is just the way I am'.

Being aware that we are not flawed, but instead adapted our thinking to make sense of our experiences by using efficient (if illogical) ways of handling the trauma, we are off the hook. It is in the split-second before the response in the event + response = outcome formula – E+R=O – where meaning is assigned and beliefs are formed. Survival reactions and UDIN moments do not provide space for pausing. We are left instead with learning in the form of a 'trauma capsule' whose purpose is to alert us to similar events in the future.

Our brain's wiring forges associations between events. In evolutionary terms, it future-proofs our safety by using past events as signposts. In this way it optimises our chances to survive another day.

Only when we take a step back to examine our reactions do we have the option insert a different filter and review the experience. If, for example, we put a blue filter over a lens, we wouldn't see the filter, but it would colour everything we saw as blue. If we change the filter, we change the experience. The new filters could be humour, imagination, self-awareness, conscience, compassion, and any number of other personal resources we could employ to reframe our experience.

With determination and a fresh approach to our thinking, we can take charge.: E + Pause → New filter → New R = New O.

| E | + | Habit Filter | New Filter | New R | = New O |
|---|---|---|---|---|---|
| Something happens | → | Automatic response (attitudes/thoughts/ perception/beliefs) <br> – culture <br> – gender <br> – emotional state | Pause - deliberate <br> – humour <br> – imagination <br> – self-awareness <br> – conscience <br> – Compassion <br> – empathy <br> – ethics | → | New experience <br> – physically <br> – emotionally <br> – behaviourally |

**Replacing the Habit Filter**

Being able to identify the origin of obstacles does not always ensure they are easily overcome. If it's something you can act on, call in the 5-Second Rule. Do one thing. Lift the phone or send that CV. It may be to seek the support of a professional; just as we seek a doctor's experience in times of illness, so, too, could we seek the support of a trained professional to unblock the less visible beliefs or obstacles that hold us back.

Let's go back to the yellow card – the warning. When something happens and we experience that flash of emotion, it is letting us know something is amiss. But instead of reacting as we did before, we can pause and take the time to understand what caused us to feel upset. We need to identify the feelings, tease out the *why* of it, and figure out with our upstairs and integrated brain what is going on inside.

The more pieces we put together, the clearer the picture and the easier to create a new and different future. Instead of flying on one wing, let's maximise our options by using all of our mental, emotional, intellectual and spiritual resources.

In real time, we can prepare for future events by planning which filter to insert, and thus resource ourselves with new approaches. When dealing with deeper issues, methods for dealing with trauma capsule beliefs or personal baggage can be found in chapters 17 and 18.

# 7 DIY Life Coaching

This chapter will provide insights that will shed light on increasing your personal and interpersonal effectiveness. It looks at how we engage with others and ourselves, and suggests ways that will increase our sense of purpose and wellbeing.

People often ask what a life coach does, and how it works. Of the numerous definitions – all of which capture some aspects – coaching is first and foremost a *process,* a way of working toward the resolution, development or achievement of an objective. Coaching works at empowering the individual to greater expressions of effectiveness. Coaches – people trained to help others increase their tennis, business or singing performance – view problems objectively by facilitating the individual to identify the gap between where they are and where they want to be, and then identifying ways to close it. The same coaching principles apply to life coaching – except, for the purposes of this book, we're talking about self-awareness coaching, both for yourself and how you might improve your relationship with others. Learning a few new skills will help you to show up more effectively in your own life, in your communications and in your ability to exert influence.

Firstly, the coach is a partner, with the responsibility to listen to what is being said and accord it equal importance to that which is happening below the radar. In this instance, we are subject and object in the process of observing ourselves. When we engage the upstairs brain, we are bringing on board our resources as a DIY coach. The DIY coach asks questions to shed light on deeper, less obvious issues. Questions unpack complexity into manageable chunks, and use all the cues, all the senses, to pick up what is being avoided or overlooked.

It requires patience and understanding, which means compassion toward ourselves and others.

Coaches listen, gather information, explore solutions, feelings, ideas and new thoughts, on the premise that the person best suited to resolve issues is not a third party, but individuals themselves. The idea behind this is that you are the expert on you. DIY coaches are solution detectives who open up a topic. They have fun with new perspectives, shining a light on possibilities. As Einstein put it, 'No problem can be solved from the same level of consciousness that created it.'

Your job as a DIY coach is to spot inconsistencies and growth potential, develop, guide and challenge yourself. Don't trudge the same old route; ask yourself questions to open up a more effective path from A to B, identify the gap between how things are and how you would like them to be, and explore the options to take you there. It's called thinking outside the box. There is no magic wand: insight is an exercise in awareness and can be learned by anyone, just as long as they are interested in expanding their growth trajectory.

We can address current limiting beliefs using past events to bring about change. This process is addressed in greater depth in later chapters on energy psychology, but it is relevant here. It is not woo-woo or OTT; it is about staying open-minded to the process. Let's take, for example, the story in the previous chapter where Pete's cat was run over, leading to the belief that his feelings did not count. As an adult, Pete could revisit that event with an open mind and without blame. He could review the scenario, knowing the response he would like to have had was one of empathy, of being heard and comforted in a way that acknowledged his loss. He cannot change his mother's response, but instead can review the event, take quiet time to reflect on what he would have wished for, and then grant himself that gift. Young Pete needed to be heard. Pete the adult could imagine picking up young

Pete, comforting him, hearing what he needed in that moment and letting him know that his feelings were important. Adult Pete could rewrite the script, allow his adult and child-self to grieve and thus allow his inner child and his adult self to unlock the 'my-feelings-don't-count' trap. There is more on this in chapters 17 and 18 and is an effective method of revising our limiting beliefs.

The potential downside of DIY coaching is that, if we're blocked on an issue, we may not be able to break out of our imprisoned thinking. But there is great satisfaction to be gained if we are able to coach ourselves through a block and come out the other side. Not only does it give us new awareness or insight, but it also builds our confidence in the long-term, allowing us to raise our game.

If your purpose is to become an empowered individual and an effective parent/colleague/friend and to learn to 'check in' with yourself regularly and attentively, you're well on your way to reconfiguring habits and engaging more effectively with others.

## It's all in the question

Any problem, project, situation or task can benefit by asking the right question. 'How are you?' is generally an ineffective question because 'Fine' reveals nothing at all but a cursory politeness by both parties. Instead, a favourite of life coaches, and a sure-fire technique to break the habit of going-nowhere questions is to consciously begin each question with WHAT.[66] The GROW model offers a range of questions in a structured sequence that will delivery results. The GROW acronym stands for the sequence of Goal, Reality, Options and Will or What Next. You may also see the model with a 'T' added to the front (TGROW), which stands for the Topic.

**Topic** –topics are too broad to achieve a good result. Asking *what specifically about the topic is the problem* uncovers the most pressing issue.

Sometimes a second or third *what specifically about* ..... digs even deeper to identify the issue.

**Goal** – establishes a specific objective. This is vital in DIY coaching - if you don't know where you are going, you will probably end up somewhere else! Asking questions helps you identify and fine-tune the main target among others, and helps to stay on track.

- What specifically do you need?
- What would you like to leave with?
- What is your longer-term goal?
- What impact will it have for you to achieve this goal?
- What would your goal look like if you achieved it – describe it

**Reality** – describe the situation as you see it – your starting point. Is the desired objective achievable? Do you know someone who has achieved this already?

- What is the current situation in detail?
- How strongly do you feel about his issue - out of 10?
- What have you done about it so far?
- What is stopping you from getting you what you want?
- What have been the outcomes?
- What stopped you from doing more?
- What obstacles are in the way?
- What supports do you need and from whom?

**Option/Obstacles/Opportunities** – provides ways of identifying pluses and minuses en route with out-of-the-box thinking that will generate useful information and allow you to decide which option is best.

- What are the different ways you could approach this?
- What options do you have?
- What else could you do? What else? What else?
- If there were no limitations what would you do?

- What resources do you need?
- What are the advantages and disadvantages of these options?

**Will/Wrap-up/What next?** – you will only be motivated to go for the goal if it resolves the issue. Prioritise and tease out the options/obstacles/opportunities. Is there a secondary gain to not achieving the goal? For instance, it may be more comfortable to remain in the current unchallenging position than take a risk that requires more effort.

- Which option will you choose?
- How does this meet your objective?
- How will you measure success?
- What could stop you achieving this?
- What support do you need? How will you get this?
- What are you key actions and what timescales do you have around these?
- What is the next step?
- When will you start this?
- On a scale of 1 to 10, rate your commitment to take this action?

Even though this is an example involving a third party, it nevertheless shows the practical application of TGROW in action. An earlier neighbourly exchange might gone like this:

Friend:  'I'm having problems with my neighbour. I feel uncomfortable with him and avoid him at all costs'

You:  'Neighbours - don't talk! Mine is from hell – which means we don't talk at all. But I also feel uncomfortable because his kids and mine play together. I make a real effort to avoid him whenever I can.'

End of conversation, or perhaps enough fuel to drive more of the same vacuous talk. You have not really listened to your friend, but have instead touched on what they have said and topped their story. The exchange serves no meaningful purpose; a hamster wheel of chat-for-chat's-sake.

A passing remark can very simply be transformed into a meaningful exchange.

Friend:  'I'm having problems with my neighbour. I feel uncomfortable with him and avoid him whenever I can' (Topic)

You:  'What's the problem?' (Goal)

Friend:  'Well, he always borrows the lawnmower and either doesn't return it or it comes back dirty with the cord all tangled' (Reality)

You:  'Is there anything you could do? – other than avoiding him, of course!' (Options)

Friend:  'I guess I need to make it clear that if he doesn't return it cleaned down with the cord neat, I won't lend it to him again.' (Options)

You:  'So do you think you'll speak to him?' (Will / wrap-up)

Friend:  'I guess so – next time he asks to borrow the mower or tools or whatever else he's on the scrounge for'

With a different focus the conversation shifted from banal to meaningful. It has enabled your friend to identify the specific issues and provides an opportunity for him to get off the treadmill of being ineffective. It provides support, shows interest, and offers the chance to be influential, exactly the sort of friend we all value in our lives.

As a more powerful communicator, you (as coach) adopt a different role with both yourself and others: you abandon the revolving door of habitual and ineffectual chat. Once a DIY coach, the conversation with a friend might go something like:

| | |
|---|---|
| Friend | I'm having difficulty with the Residents' Association meetings. I've been chair twice and I haven't any control. I need to stay on track, otherwise it goes on forever! |
| You | OK - tell me, what is it you want to achieve? (Topic). |
| Friend | Well, the meetings so far have been pretty chaotic. They run on and on and we aren't making much progress. I don't know how to keep control. (Goal) |
| You | OK, so it's about being in control? Describe to me what it would look like, in practical terms, what a successful meeting would look like? |
| Friend | First, that it only lasts an hour – not two or three. (Goal 1) |
| You | Anything else? |
| Friend | I would set an agenda and stick to it, not go around the houses with everyone throwing in their ten cents' worth or hearing everyone's anecdotes. (Goal 2) |
| You | Anything else for this perfect meeting? |
| Friend | Yes, we would know clearly what actions will be taken and by whom. (Goal 3) |
| You | OK, tell me now what's actually been happening so far. (Reality) |
| Friend | We overrun, often by an hour or two, and still don't come out with anything concrete. Afterwards I feel we haven't achieved anything. I'm inexperienced. I mean, what does a check-out know about chairing meetings! |

| You | Tell me more about how you set your agenda. |
| Friend | Well, when I email everyone with notice of the meeting, I also ask for ideas on top of the usual – you know, the garden contractors, cleaning the open spaces, street lighting - the usual |
| You | OK, so what could you do differently? (Option) |
| Friend | Now that I've described it, it seems obvious! I could spend the first five minutes confirming the agenda. I could ask each resident what he or she thinks we need to cover. |
| You | What else? (More options) |
| Friend | Also allocating time blocks to each item. That way I know how the hour is panning out and when we need to speed things up. I need to make sure any action steps are clear, so we all know who's doing what. |
| You | How could you do that? (Option / Will) |
| Friend | I could put my watch on the table so I can keep track of time easily. And record any action points so that I can summarise at the end. |
| You | Let's get this down on paper as an action plan. What action items are you going to commit to? Write them down as you tell me. (Will or What Next) |
| Friend | 1) First five minutes to set the agenda |
| | 2) Agree on time allocation |
| | 3) Make sure I can see the time to track our progress. |
| | 4) Clarify each action item and who will be doing it. I'll try this and see how it goes. |

## Communicating more effectively

As illustrated, a simple structure such as the GROW model can truly change the nature of your communications and relationships. It places the focus on the other person or on the issue at hand, and is a skill that can be learned through practice. New skills and updated tools help us do a better job. The main tool is listening – to yourself and others. What lies behind the words?, the lump in your throat or the lump in theirs? If you sense an inconsistency, then there almost certainly is one. Observe yourself – not as a critic, but as a mentor or champion with your or their highest interests at heart. Know that the intelligent being you are has a rationale for everything, even though it may not be apparent or may appear illogical; your reasons lie in the complex and often contradictory mind of the child conditioned by someone else's agenda or random significant event. Stop yourself in the pendulum swing between left and right or downstairs/upstairs brains. Find the middle ground.

The person who communicates effectively is self-aware. They operate from a mind-set of self-sufficiency and groundedness, consider their own and the needs of others, take responsibility for their mistakes and successes, are humble about their strengths, refrain from thoughtlessness, and are aware of how their words and actions affect others. They don't occupy the high moral ground. They do not need to be right or be on the defensive. They do not need to win at any cost. They listen and respond, respecting their own and others' viewpoints.

So whether it's with a third party or in conversation with yourself, ask what could be done differently?, what specifically is the problem?, what have I tried that failed?, what other resources could I use?, what is the elephant in the room?, who has the expert knowledge I need to take it to the next level? Questions such as these open up possibilities that are otherwise shut down by past habits.

The difference between a chat and a coaching conversation is based on questions. Those to avoid usually start with 'Why' or 'How'. 'Why did I/you . . . ?' questions frequently elicit justifications, excuses or defensiveness because of an implied criticism. 'How' questions invariably evoke analytical or philosophical answers – responses directly from the thinking mind that is trapped in a loop of habit. The answers might be interesting, but they do not allow forward movement, insight or resolution.

Instead of asking, 'How did the exam go?' and getting a monosyllabic 'Fine' or 'Good' from your fifteen year old, start with the magical WHAT. 'What part of your preparation was most helpful?' or 'What part of the exam was the most challenging?' This forces the person (or yourself) to review what they did using a higher-order process that will inform the preparation or approach for future exams. Who would not want the richer exchange?

'What do you want to achieve?' or 'What else could you try?' or 'What do you need to do next?' draws the conversation toward a solution. It may be important to know the status of the problem by asking why or how, but movement is created *not* by being sucked into the vortex of the problem, but by throwing the process in the direction of the solution.

Instead of, 'I'm late again' ask, 'What do I need to do next time to be on time?': it forces cause-and-effect thinking so that you can identify the obstacles to be planned for in the future. Instead of asking why something went wrong, ask what could be done differently next time. Good questions force a brainstorm that tracks the steps which led to the stalemate, and opens the gates for fresh thinking. Success and failure both have a structure: once the real issue is apparent, corrective action can be deliberate and planned in preparation for the next stage.

DIY life coaches should not be deterred from learning a few techniques to use in everyday interactions. Insights that add value to efficiency at work, at home or in our communities can only be good. It's all down to curiosity and the questions we ask, where good questions make for good solutions. Instead of being judgemental or being one up, we get a lot further if we let the judge and jury stay out. Curiosity elicits valuable information. Our own resources frequently contain the solution, or the potential for one.

## Changing from the inside out

Let's start by being attentive to our emotions, gut feelings, and the subtle and often neglected language of the body and its reactions.

Once we grasp the idea that we can be change-agents in our own and others' lives, it is important to be alert and willing to learn from our shortcomings and disappointments. In other words, we should never regard these as failures, but as opportunities for learning and growth. It's called feedback.

When we say, 'It was stupid of me, but I can't help doing. . .' , the critical voice is really that of a scolding parent. Instead of passing judgment, try to figure out what the advantage was in the unwanted behaviour. In other words, take a few moments to discover what we might have gained from our actions – the secondary gain. Was it approval? A sense of power? Avoiding punishment? Once we exercise compassion and give ourselves credit for being smart enough to have survived, we may understand what purpose the unwanted behaviour served. Since it has raised its head, it may well be something we have outgrown.

Here are some areas to focus on to begin changing from the inside out:

**Don't pass judgement:** When we pass judgement on ourselves, we draw a line and park our disappointment on the 'wrong' side. From that position we no longer exercise curiosity and may, instead, condemn ourselves and lose the feedback that holds the answer. On the assumption that we are intelligent, as we all are, pause and ask what we could have done differently. Future-proof yourself. Be deliberate. Be curious. Sow a seed and nurture its growth.

**Look out for yellow card warnings:** Be aware that feelings don't 'just happen'. Recognise the advance warning, the yellow card, the tell-tale spasm, comments from others, gut instinct or intuition that alert you to what's going on. Learn to trust these flashes as advanced warning signals. It is the body providing feedback that something is out of sync. Pause. Take a moment to do a reality check and decide on your next move.

**Do something every day that helps build your confidence:** The more we build self-respect and begin to trust ourselves, the more our confidence grows. The more it grows, the greater our sense of self and our integrity in the minds of others. If someone kept breaking their promise to you or letting you down, you'd soon give up on them. Make sure you stop doing it to yourself and build your confidence one act, one deliberate step at a time. Make it count. Acknowledge even small achievements and be proud on the inside. Building confidence is like building muscle – the more you exercise it, the stronger the muscle memory becomes. Recognise the things on which you can deliver, and reward yourself when you do. Small gains and banking successes establishes a foundation for bigger gains – remember the 5:1 ratio? That's how you build your confidence – one success, one instalment at a time.

**Decide how much you want on your plate:** Having too much on your plate can be overwhelming, leading to stress or overload. In balance, stress is what keeps us on our toes, sharpens our concentration, or drives us to study for an exam when we'd rather be watching TV. This good stress has a name – eustress. Too little stimulation and we lack motivation. Too much and our performance becomes impaired. The optimal point where our behaviour and stimulation are stretched but not overloaded - being in the zone – is at the top of the bell-shaped curve in the diagram below. Beyond the tipping point, stress stops being helpful and starts to cause damage to our minds and bodies. Saying yes to everything comes at a price.

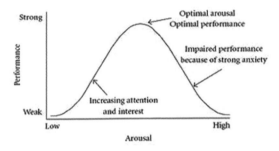

**Bell-shaped curve showing optimal performance and stress**

**Watch your internal dialogue:** Internal dialogue, the conversations we have inside our heads, affects us as much as if it were said out loud by somebody else. Truly – would you keep a friend who spoke to you the way you speak to yourself? Repetition reinforces the belief, and when it is negative, as it frequently is, the detrimental effect is cumulative. Remember Hebb's Law that neurons that fire together wire together? Whether it's someone else or your own voice reminding you *how stupid you were to have* . . ., or. . . or . . . it's the fuel that stokes the beliefs that keep us stuck. It's time to stop. It's time to change the message.

If your purpose is to become a more effective individual/ parent/ colleague/friend, you will need to 'check in' with yourself regularly and attentively, and be willing to unlearn those things that retard your growth.

Make a conscious decision to observe which part of your brain is calling the shots. Consider what you could do differently next time – called 'next time thinking'. Bring together the rich resources of your whole brain. That is how to increase effectiveness and gain a reputation for being influential. Take one and then another step on your wellbeing journey.

# Section 3 Mind

The history of our individual experience determines what the mind perceives and interprets. The same event may be experienced differently by individuals, communities or nations. In other words, is what I see and what you see the same? Technically, yes. The senses are bombarded with information, which send stimuli to the brain. It is how we interpret it through the filter of experience that shapes the outcome, whether actively and passively employed.

Experientially, and from testimony, it often appears that two people had witnessed different events. This is because my filters, such as all-or-nothing thinking, overgeneralising, negative bias or catastrophising, or my role as driver rather than as a passenger involved in a vehicle collision, differ. As would the interpretation by the driver or passenger in the other car. Just as identical twins with the same genetic heritage will have different life experiences, so, too, will each differ in the way they interpret events.

Mind is the brain at work, the brain in action, responsible for how we interpret the world. This section looks at how the mind is formed, how it works and how consciousness and experience can be entry points to bring about change.

# 8 The Learning Process

## Early Learning Development

Learning in our early years sets the trajectory for our lives. Developmental psychology follows the lifespan through infancy, adolescence, adulthood and ageing, but originally focussed on development during childhood as the period when the most change occurred. Early development theorists explored different aspects, with Piaget looking at cognitive states, Erikson at psychological states, Vygotsky at the social interaction in the development of cognition and Bowlby positing that children come into the world biologically pre-programmed to form attachments.[67] In other words, there is no single account of early learning and development. What we do know, however, is that children learn by experience, observing, copying, being rewarded and punished, rather than by developing a hypothesis, testing it and revising their initial thinking.

Until the 1980s it was understood that we were born with what early philosophers and psychologists called a *tabula rasa* – the mind as a blank slate, unruffled by beliefs imprinted by how the world operates. It emphasised the individual's character and identity as fixed; human nature was seen as immutable.

I recall hearing the story of a pumpkin in the shape of a watering can that was on display at a country fair. 'How did you do that?', asked spectators. 'It was easy', said the farmer, 'all I did was plant the seed in a glass watering can. I fed and watered it like all the other pumpkins. When it was fully grown, I broke the glass with a hammer, and *voilà*, a watering-can-shaped pumpkin.

Just as that pumpkin grew according to the limits of its environment, so were we shaped by our family, school, who we hung out with, our neighbourhood, religion and culture. Though the watering-can pumpkin can do nothing about its shape, the same is NOT true for us.

The belief that we are stuck being who we are has changed with advances in understanding the brain and the mind. The wonderful thing about being human is our capacity to learn. Who we think we are is who we were programmed and rewarded and punished to be. All learning, everything that has shaped us to this point, **can be unlearned.**[68] With new and more effective thoughts, beliefs and behaviours, and by taking responsibility for re-visioning our lives, we can alter our course. Eliminating what no longer serves us and choosing to do things differently is how we reshape our futures.

This understanding of the mind is related to the phenomenon of *brain plasticity*, the brain's ability to reorganise itself by growing new or pruning old brain cells and connections. It's a phenomenon that opens exciting doors. Advances in neurobiology and neuroscience demonstrate that we can, without restriction, reshape experience by reviewing the input and output of our sensory processing. As we have learned, change starts with an Event, our Response to it, leading to an Outcome – the revisiting of E + R = O.

We are born with all the brain cells we need, but mostly they are unconnected. However, studies have demonstrated that foetal rats exposed to Mozart were better at solving maze problems later in life, and babies exposed to the sound of a dog barking while still in the womb did not startle at the sound as newborns.[69] These and other studies show that learning (cognition) and therefore brain cell connections are formed in the womb once the biological prerequisite, in these cases hearing, has been reached. Evidence shows that the unborn child learns the sound of its mother's voice, recognises theme tunes from

TV soaps, and shows preferences for tastes and smells according to the variety of environmental information recorded.

More significant than the sound of a voice or theme tune are the influences flooding the baby's body from the mother's diet, stress levels and drug or pharmaceutical use, factors that condition the baby for life beyond the womb. The baby's and mother's physiology, while separate, are one, for everything that enters the mother's bloodstream passes through the placenta to the foetus, including nicotine, alcohol or stress hormones. This is exemplified, tragically, in babies of drug addict mothers born drug dependent, or in highly stressed mothers whose brains and bodies frequently shift into crisis mode and flood the foetus with increased levels of adrenaline and cortisol – less than optimal conditions for an unborn baby.

The foetal and early childhood environments are, therefore, significant. With no ill-will intended, parents or guardians may be unaware of their role in shaping the baby's life trajectory by, for example, the habit of passivity or aggression, self-sabotage or self-defeating patterns, passive hostility, instant gratification, self-destructive thoughts, violent aggression or other psychologically unhealthy states.

Like blotting paper, we absorb the ink spills of our environment. As we develop, we adapt our behaviour according to the rewards and punishments doled out by others, which, remember, are often a product of *their* learning. The family/school/religion/neighbourhood environments in which we find ourselves – the scaffolding of rules and taboos – are what 'domesticate' us into believing that we must play the hand we have been dealt, and that nothing and no one can change it. We believe we are who we are – the product of all the messages we have consciously and unconsciously absorbed and the rules by which we play – no matter how unjust they are perceived to be.

Baby and adult brains have roughly the same number of neurons: around 100 billion. What babies lack are the connecting branches, which develop and grow over time. With repeated experience and the resulting associations, neurons wire up to create important pathways to various centres of the brain. Because an estimated 90% to 95% of brain cells are organised and connect in the first five to seven years, it is important not to underestimate the significance of these early years in a child's life.[70]

The Jesuit maxim, 'Give me a boy for his first seven years and I'll give you the man' acknowledges the significance of these early years in shaping us. Children will have been exposed to a great deal by the age of seven, before they have acquired the capacity for critical thinking. They learn from listening to and watching their parents, siblings, relatives, teachers, cartoon characters, TV and sports stars, peers and community leaders. Indeed, more than 90% of how we live our lives is run by the programmes (the beliefs, habits, behaviours, emotional reactions, attitudes) and unconscious states downloaded in those early years.[71] Indeed, the ACE Study mentioned below that all this happens by the age of four and not seven – an even shorter timeframe. The ACE Study confirms what we know instinctively: the greater the adversity and the earlier the impact, the more serious the consequences on the child's health, behaviour and life potential.[72] The Jesuits knew something studies have now confirmed: the quality of the early developmental environment has implications for the resilience and life potential of every child.

Three types of stress shape the potential for resilience: **eustress** or positive stress – where, for example, a child falls down and picks herself up. In this case, she learns that by her actions she can overcome challenges. Perceiving stress in this way grows out of strong attachment, secure, safe or loving home and supportive school environments, which provide a stability that allows the child to return to balance. **Stress** in circumstances like war zones or dysfunctional neighbourhoods can be stabilised by the influence of a strong and reliable family connection or other champion. **Toxic** or **chronic stress** happens when the child experiences elevated exposure to stress without the protection of a stable family, or where the family, itself, is the source of the stress (as in parental violence, abuse or neglect). Once the fight, freeze or flight system is permanently 'on', chronic stress becomes the norm and the child will be edgy and nervous, seeing the world as an unsafe or hostile place.[73]

## ACES – Adverse Childhood Experience Study[74]

A significant research study, the Adverse Childhood Experience Study commenced in 1989. It was designed to analyse the relationship between childhood trauma and the risk of physical and mental illness in adulthood. Over the course of two decades, the results demonstrated a strong, graded relationship between the level of traumatic stress in childhood and poor physical, mental and behavioural outcomes later in life. This potent combination of high ACE scores and early brain development in a child significantly affected cognitive and executive brain function in later life.

A sample of the risk factors considered in this long-term retrospective study is given below.

–   Recurring physical abuse
–   Recurring emotional abuse
–   Sexual abuse
–   An alcohol and/or drug abuser in the household
–   An incarcerated household member
–   Family member who is chronically depressed, mentally ill, institutionalized, or suicidal

- Mother is treated violently
- One or no parents
- Physical neglect
- Emotional neglect

Over 17,000, mostly middle income American children, up to age 18 who grew up experiencing increments of these adverse conditions, were found to exhibit chronic health problems and impaired mental health and wellbeing. The cumulative effect led to negative measures relating to disease, obesity, addiction, unemployment, education and crime. Many of us can identify one or more factors from the list above within our own upbringing that were not ideal, some of which we survived and others which left more indelible marks. However, not everyone is affected in the same way, which raises the question: what are the factors that make the difference between those with impaired health and wellbeing and those who escaped the predicted consequences to achieve success?

## Overcoming Adversity

It has long been shown that nurturing may be the most significant contribution parents provide to their children's wellbeing, identified by researchers as the 'super variable',[75] where children's emotional maturation provides a foundation upon which later social development takes place. The catalyst seems to lie in the child having at least one champion; a person who provided support enough for the child to develop a stable core. Those who have risen above early adversity to re-invent themselves had a devoted mother or other nurturing caregiver who compensated for the adversity. A peek into the early lives of some public figures gives credence to the theory.

TV star Oprah Winfrey says, 'I don't think of myself as a poor deprived ghetto girl who made good. I think of myself as somebody who, from an early age, knew I was responsible for myself and had to make good.' An impoverished urban lifestyle had its negative effect on Winfrey as a young teenager, and her problems were compounded by repeated sexual abuse, starting at age nine. She was returned to her father, who, she claimed, saved her life. He was very strict but provided her with guidance, structure, rules, and books. Another champion was her fourth grade teacher, Mrs. Duncan, who helped her conquer her fear and encouraged her many talents.[76]

Former US President Bill Clinton's mother was 6 months pregnant when his father died. He was sent to live with his grandparents, both of whom lavished attention on him until aged four, and who instilled in him the importance of a good education. From age four to fifteen he returned to live with his mother and abusive and alcoholic stepfather in terrible poverty.[77]

Barack Obama was raised by his single mother who later married and then separated from his Kenyan father at age two. Aged four, he moved with his mother and new stepfather to Indonesia. Struggling to reconcile the perceptions of his mixed-race heritage and other challenges, aged ten he returned to Honolulu to his maternal grandparents, who championed him to adulthood.[78]

The tragic example of extreme adversity in the absence of a nurturing champion results in an altogether different high-achiever's life trajectory:

- His father died when his mother was 4 months pregnant
- His twelve year old brother died of cancer two months later
- His mother suffered major depression and tried unsuccessfully to abort him
- She then tried to kill herself
- Soon after birth he was given away to an uncle, a retired army officer

- At age three the young boy was returned to his mother
- He was physically and psychologically abused by his stepfather
- At age ten he ran away to the safety of his uncle's home

We have all heard of this man, whose life circumstances appear to have offered very little in the form of nurturing, championing or sanctuary. His name: Saddam Hussein.[79]

These examples are not an attempt to generalise, but rather to illustrate what psychology suggests are necessary prerequisites for us to thrive. The take-away message is that early adversity can be reversed. Hebb's Law – neurons that fire together, wire together, reverberates with the message that adversity **can be overcome**: as adults, if we are not our own champion, then who will be? It is a role we can and must take on for ourselves if we are to enjoy growth and wellbeing.

## What we can change, and what we can't

The diagram on the next page is a model of the nature-nurture debate. There is no agreement on where the limits of 1st Nature are – are heart disease or cancer inherited? – but this model illustrates our make-up, with those aspects of our character that are inherited on the left, and the rest, which we can influence, on the right.

Standing at five foot tall and a light complexion, you could wager your socks that my parents weren't six footers, and that they were both Caucasian. The genetic aspects of inheritance are the 'givens', the physical aspects that are contained in the DNA of our inherited genetic pools. Just about all the rest, it is argued by many, is up for grabs. The fact that I have Aunt Dorothy's legs – and they weren't her best feature – means I'm stuck with them. Just about everything else – my personality, my sociable-ness or my inclination to comply or rebel – seems part of me, but are actually learned, survival behaviours. You may argue that many of our predispositions are our genetic inheritance, for example that heart disease runs in the family, but more will be said in relation to our genetic inheritance in chapter 13.

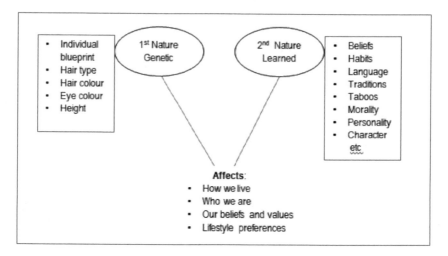

**Model of Nature-Nurture**

The Law of Repetition was described long ago by Aristotle, and is the same as Hebb's Law. If we repeat thought or behaviour patterns, brain connections are reinforced and strengthened to become what is familiar. Once established, the thought or behaviour happens automatically. An opinion expressed often enough becomes a truth, habit or belief, when it is, in reality, a construct of the mind. However, once set, it guides and defines who we are, what we are capable of and determines the height of the bar we set – usually well below our potential. Remember the limiting belief of our ancestors that the world was flat? For how long did it control how far they could sail before they came to believe something different? We need to be alert to the presence of 'flat-world' thinking of our own that limits our potential.

State something often enough and we remember it: two times two equals four. In just the same way, 'You're no good at singing' becomes hardwired to 'I'm no good at singing', 'He's shy' becomes 'I'm shy'. Having practiced it aloud or in our minds, or having heard it stated again and again by others, it has become a belief we've taken on, whether true or not. And tragically, the truths we've absorbed, the compasses by which we navigate our lives, continue to control us even though they may have exceeded their usefulness.

Let's offer ourselves the possibility that some of the truths we hold, based on the opinion of others and formed as small children,, might have a shelf life that has long past it sell-by date. After all, what adult would hand over the control of their life to the 'small child' version of themselves?

Within your early years, the approval or disapproval, put ups and put downs, and the overt or subtle acceptance or rejection by those with authority were doled out for your 'benefit'. Who you think you are is who you were programmed or *conditioned* to be. Conditioning is everything you learned and adapted to in the early years as a direct response to the rewards, punishments or opinions from multiple sources.

As the bright and innocent child, you thrived or survived by doing more of what you were rewarded to do or be, survival being a primal drive. Rewards and punishments were handed out to lure you into doing what others wanted. You learned the rules. You adapted your behaviour to fit in with the expectations and agendas of those you relied on, and paid the price for their approval.

No one else but you are the expert on you. Even if your head is telling you one thing, your body will let you know when something is amiss. Now, instead of defaulting to what is *reasonable* as a result of how you were trained, trust your body, no matter how insignificant the signal might feel. Your stomach might knot or your breathing might catch – this is you giving you an unconscious body-mind yellow card that something is out of kilter.

Resentment or embarrassment or guilt is feedback from your body that signals you to press the pause button *before* R. Take a moment to reflect. Start to trust your inner wisdom. It may not be easy to stand up for, or begin to acknowledge, your authentic self. After all, you've been practising a different way for years. But jump. Make the choice. Shed the old ways as you would an out-of-date garment, and replace it with something you'd be proud to wear and that others might admire.

Ways in which we can break the mould and do something different to release our authentic selves is to run an audit of the things we like and do not like about our lives.

— What do I want to do more of?
— What do I want to do less of?
— What I would like to begin?
— What I would like to stop?
— Who would I like to get to know better?
— With whom would I like to spend less more or less time?

Am I happy with . . .

— The people I hang out with?
— How I communicate?
— The job/education/training I'm doing?
— My command of English?
— The level of education I have reached?
— The kind of friend I am?
— My timekeeping?
— My talkativeness or the ways in which I express myself?

- The role model I am to others?
- How well I know or understand my neighbours or the people in my community?

Being aware, proactive and taking deliberate action is the first step to overcoming the limits imposed by your seven-year old self. Allow yourself the chance to understand not just *what* you are feeling, but WHY. What's behind the anger? Is it years of hurt, disappointment or frustration? Answers to questions such as these reveal the true nature of our resistance, and are all 2nd Nature. All are *learned* and can be unlearned and replaced with something more rewarding. Isn't that an exciting prospect and a positive place from which to venture into greater wellbeing?

# 9 Change Starts with the Mind

This chapter looks at how we short-change ourselves before giving ourselves a chance. Under optimal conditions, the mind has the potential to identify ways to overcome limits. Our tendency, though, is to ignore the prompts, give out and give up, and continue ploughing the same furrow. However, when we adopt an open mindset we free ourselves up to appreciate the value of feedback we had previously ignored and learn from our mistakes.

## Placebo and Nocebo Effects

Research shows that placebo and nocebo effects stem from processes occurring in the brain,[80] where expectation, belief, conditioning and subconscious associations set us up to believe that this or that outcome will occur. In other words, belief alone can make a difference to the outcome. The mind is that powerful.

In clinical trials, patients are randomly assigned to three groups: experimental, control and placebo groups, and the gold standard of medical research. The experimental group receives, for example, an active drug, the placebo group receives a sugar pill, and the control group receives nothing. Robustly controlled clinical trials invariably report changes in those subjects assigned to the placebo group in spite of there being no active substance in the drug, or, in the case of surgery, no corrective procedure having been carried out.[81]

A placebo is anything that seems to be a 'real' medical treatment, but isn't. It could be a pill, an injection or some other type of fake treatment such as surgery. What all placebos have in common is that they do not contain an active ingredient or involve a procedure meant to affect health.

The dark side of the placebo is the *nocebo* effect. It may occur when the patient is given a sugar pill or undergoes some other fake treatment, but is told the drug has terrible side effects. Just knowing the risks may produce the side effect or negatively impact the patient's recovery. In addition to medical research, the nocebo effect has also been documented in cases of voodoo, where cultural belief in a witch doctor's hex can cause illness or death with no evidence of injury, disease or poison.[82]

Being aware of how our thoughts may shape outcomes, our best interests are served when we take into account their consequences. The diagram below illustrates how actions, thoughts, beliefs and habits lead to and strengthen our self-image, which, in turn, reinforce the status quo.

Beck's Cognitive Triad (1976), is a psychological model of how spontaneous thoughts about the Self, the World and the Future conspire to determine our life experience from a psychological point of view. In other words each aspect of the triangle informs and is influenced by the others in a cycle of self-fulfilment. For example, if you view yourself as a glass-half-full person, your view of the future and the world will mirror those qualities. Feelings of distrust and fear about the world will have implications for growth and personal effectiveness.

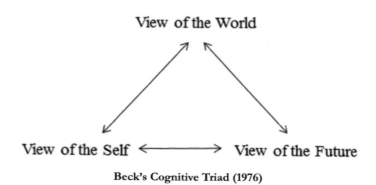

**View of the World**

**View of the Self** ⟷ **View of the Future**

**Beck's Cognitive Triad (1976)**

The Self-Talk Cycle below confirms Beck's self-fulfilling prophecy. If I hold the belief that 'I'm no good at maths', when faced with a maths problem I will almost certainly avoid it. This may determine how I respond when faced with calculating value for money of different products in the supermarket. I may not even try because 'I know what I know about myself.'

Actions, attitudes and habits lead to, strengthen and build the belief we hold about ourselves: our self-image. Our self-image, in turn, predicts how we behave or act. It also shapes how we filter input. How we think or act becomes a learned 'truth' and subsequently a self-fulfilling prophecy.

**Self-Talk Cycle**

Hidden in this model is a startling tool for change; but more on that later. Let's look at the structure of how talking to ourselves reinforces our self-image, then determines the way we behave.

Usually when we make a decision, we start on the left of the diagram above – with actions/behaviour/beliefs/habits. If our decision is to lose weight, we rethink our diet and our supermarket shopping habits, determined to plan the menu for the week and shop accordingly. We join a gym, buy a new pair of trainers for that half-hour run before breakfast. But before long, the old habits creep in and our trolley looks like it did four months ago and our runners, well . . . We stand back, exasperated at our lack of resolve or find legitimate reasons why we couldn't continue with the regime. The image we hold of ourselves may be of 'not having enough willpower'. With an ah-what-the-heck attitude, we tuck into a croissant and latte as we settle into the start of a new day. There is more on willpower on page 114.

When we berate ourselves for making a mistake, we take on the role of a scolding parent – and who ever listened to them? So instead of falling prey to the belief that we have no willpower, we can choose instead to believe that *there is no such thing as failure, only feedback.* If we give up on ourselves, we not only lose the lesson, but find ourselves once more on the treadmill of failure. Let's pause, reframe our thoughts and use all of our brain.

Success and failure have a structure. Break the problem down to its constituent parts and analyse what could be done differently next time. Instead of seeing a missed goal as failure, monitor, evaluate and adjust the plan to more closely align with your goal. Experiential learning is hands-on, trial and error or learning-by-doing, illustrated in this adaptation of Kolb's Experiential Learning Cycle.[83]

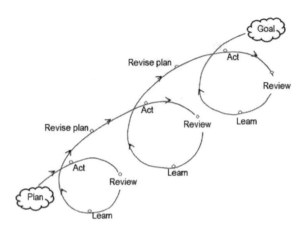

**Adaptation of Kolb's Learning Cycle**

The idea behind it is that when we do something, we need to participate in the process by checking to see if it brought us closer to, or further from, where we had hoped to be. By tracking and evaluating what led to the less-than-satisfactory outcome, we can make adjustments so that our next attempt will bring us closer to our goal. With each successive and successful attempt, we are one step closer to what we want. If we have deviated, we can quickly work out what went wrong and correct it for next time.

Take a learner driver attempting a three-point turn or a gymnast getting to grips with a tricky parallel bar routine. After numerous attempts they will have mastered their respective manoeuvres using feedback. Experiential learning – learning by doing – can be applied to our interactions with others, to managing our quick temper, or to making sure we arrive on time. Awareness applied to changing a bad habit requires as much commitment and practice as does any manual skill.

Let us never forget how we applaud a baby taking its first steps, not just once, but each time they add to their success. The message here is simple: we need to acknowledge and celebrate each gain we make, no matter how small. Even as adults we need championing. We *must* honour our achievements – take pride in them. Not by flaunting them publicly, but by the deep down, private satisfaction of a job well done. Make every success count. This method exercised in Japan's competitive manufacturing industry is called *kaizen,* or continuous improvement. Learning from mistakes works as well with car manufacture as it does with bad habits or new skills.

Our job is to review the process and install the learning BEFORE the next time. In this way our thinking has been primed for improvement. Whether to minimise mistakes or maximise success, feedback is invaluable for learning and growing to change the internal blueprint.

## Recipe for Change

You will notice that the diagram on the next page, the Change Cycle, is exactly the same as the Self-talk Cycle on page 111. It is within this model that the magic lies. Failure is guaranteed if we begin on the left in the self-talk cycle referred to earlier, proven by many failed New Year resolutions. Trying to change the belief or habit is not sustainable because it relies on plotting a new course using the old map. We have to start instead by drafting a new map, the *self-image* box on the right in the same diagram as the start point. Exercising control over the image you wish to create means eliminating the behaviours or habits you with to change. By determining a new you, a new path or belief, you are changing everything that cascaded automatically from the old you.

**Change Cycle**

Don't wait until you have more willpower or your next birthday - plant the seed and see it bear fruit in your mind long before it manifests. Set yourself small goals – not to be late, to follow through on your promise, to say no when you mean no. Think it through in your mind so that you have a plan. If the plan is not fit for purpose, revise it using feedback.

Do not dump the plan just because it didn't work. Begin to legitimise yourself as a person of honour, for if you don't, who will? You wouldn't trust someone who constantly broke their word to you, would you, yet we do it to ourselves time and again. Begin by taking full responsibility for your actions: rewrite who you want to become. Without action, nothing will change.

Change does not happen overnight, but takes sustained effort and determination. If change was easy, we would all look and feel healthy, be happy, have given up smoking/diet Coke/chocolate and the bathroom scale. When we find we have slipped back into the old way,, simply acknowledge it, use feedback to understand why or what, and once more align your purpose with your goal.

For example, instead of continuing with the belief that *I'm no good at maths,* engage your brain. You might ask: *I wonder if I could get what maths is all about? Maybe it was the teacher who failed me by not explaining the basics in a way I could understand. Having missed out on the basics – no wonder all the subsequent years were difficult. Perhaps it wasn't that I was bad at maths. I know I'm smart in other areas - maybe I just didn't understand/ was distracted/ the teacher didn't explain it in a way that I understood 'cos the other kids got it.*

Get the message? Press the pause button. Review the 'facts' and surprise yourself with a fresh perspective. Reframing a problem invariably connects up the dots differently. Changing a habit can be simple, but not necessarily easy. The right hand side of the Cycle of Change diagram is your new starting point.

Awareness and the will to change are pre-requisites. Once in the starting blocks, we must keep an eye on the solution, not the problem, if we are to avoid the pitfalls. We have it in us to open the door to a fresh start. And we have our internal dialogue:

1. Allow yourself to believe that change is possible;

2. Identify and name what you want and what you aspire to;

3. Practice.

New ways shape new destinations. They shape new lives. Take 100% responsibility for everything you do and be your own champion. Success is relative, where a small step for you may be a giant step for another. Going to literacy classes might be as big a step for A as filling in the CAO form is for B. It therefore doesn't give a measure of your worth to compare your achievements with those of others. A better index is how much effort, persistence or commitment you demonstrate. Instead of finding reasons why the project, savings plan or diet didn't succeed, use feedback to understand what you could do differently and reset your course. Become your own team leader.

Taking responsibility requires you to understand that the filters you unconsciously use were forged, you may recall, in your formative years. The trouble with filters is they have a profound influence on perception. They can shut off the ability to take in the good news or see the issue from a different angle. You cannot change events or history, but can review the filters you use. Taking responsibility means the buck stops with you, and the concept applies both to success and failure. If you were not alone but part of a team, then take responsibility for your part in the success or failure of the project.

Every new invention starts with an idea, the vision of what the inventor hopes to achieve. Bring the creative, emotional and team leader parts of your brain together and give them space to communicate. Let's raise the possibility that new understanding can open the door to overcoming our limitations. How exciting would that be! After all, Edison is quoted as saying, 'I did not fail with the light bulb. I just found 10,000 ways that it didn't work'. Doesn't this exemplify the exciting power and potential for incremental change from feedback, starting with yourself as you are today?

# 10 Comfort Zones and Effectiveness

Building on what we discussed in the previous chapter about taking personal responsibility and the potential for change, this chapter will give an understanding of what a comfort zone (CZ) is, and how awareness of CZs can support our journey. It also looks at areas where we can exercise more control and thereby exert greater influence.

CZs are a challenge: it's not that we're inherently lazy, it's just that human nature is always on the lookout for the quickest and easiest way to get what it wants. Ever noticed how we repeat the same things over and over, even when not in our best interests? This is driven by our desire for a short-term gain or quick fix. Outmanoeuvred by our ability to resist the physical, emotional or psychological cues, we fall prey to the *same old, same old*. These default safe havens are our CZs.

The concept of a comfort zone (CZ) is both simple and complex. CZs can be helpful and they can be limiting. Helpful for the public speaker who confidently stands up to address a gathering. Limiting, when a hi-tech company with a reliable product is so complacent that it fails to innovate and thus loses market share to competitors. CZs are very real. They are everywhere.

We have individual, family, gender, religious, neighbourhood, school, indeed, an infinite number of CZs. Each belief we hold has its own limits of what we find acceptable or not. How we dress. With whom we associate. What foods we eat. We have comfort zones about what newspapers we do or don't read. We even have CZs about holiday destinations, or whether bikinis should be worn by the over-fifties.

Everything we have an opinion on, every belief we hold and everything we perceive through our senses of taste, touch, sight, smell and feel, has its own bandwidth of tolerance. Overwhelming, isn't it?

## Bandwidth of Tolerance

Homo sapiens and the animal kingdom have many things in common: when hungry, we eat or, when threatened, we take flight, flee or freeze. We know by now from earlier chapters how the body responds to stressors: by releasing neurotransmitters into the bloodstream which alert us to a threat or opportunity. Our body responds physiologically through measuring blood pressure, pulse, respiration or skin conductivity. If you were to imagine crossing a crocodile-infested river by means of a dodgy rope bridge, your heart would surely race, your muscles tense and your breathing change. All these clues are the body's way of telling you that you are out of your CZ; its self-preservation alert encourages you to avoid the risk and retreat to your place of safety.

An antelope grazing is in balance. When it perceives a predator, its system is flooded with hormones to fuel its escape. With the danger over and the fuel spent, the antelope returns to grazing. Anyone who has watched wildlife films will have noticed how quickly balance is restored.

Exactly like the high and low cut-off limits of a thermostat, we fluctuate and adjust our thoughts or behaviour to maintain equanimity within our own pre-set parameters. Your tolerances will be different from mine and almost everyone else's. Being creatures of comfort, we are wired to resolve feelings of discomfort; we return to 'normal' by way of retreating to where everything feels *right* once again. Homeostasis is that balance, the comfortable place or state of ease.

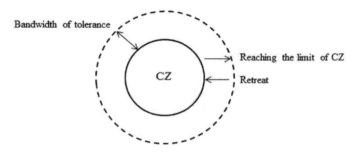

Bandwidth of tolerance

CZ

Reaching the limit of CZ

Retreat

**How our comfort zone operates when we reach its limit**

Our systems are mobilised in much the same way. However, unlike the antelope, whose trigger is always an external threat, you and I have the ability to turn on the fight-or-flight response with thoughts of future or past events. We also have the ability to replay events again and again. At the first hint of threat, neurochemicals are released whether the stressful event is real or is a story being replayed in our heads. But, unlike the antelope, we do not burn off the hormones during our burst to outrun the threat. The 'fire alarm' in our brain, the amygdala, reacts to triggers, real or imagined, just as the smoke alarm in your kitchen cannot differentiate between burnt toast or the house being ablaze. There is no discernment: it is either on or off.

The major stress hormone, cortisol, is public health enemy number one. With the body primed for action that doesn't happen, the system remains flooded with accumulated stress hormones, with consequential health risks. The case for not only taking your foot off the accelerator, but allowing time for meditation or other relaxation practice, is to allow the body the opportunity to recover. An analogy could be when one cup, then another of salt is added to a basin of water, the basin will soon become undrinkable. However, if the basin is frequently replenished with fresh water, one cup of salt will have little effect.

## Creating New Comfort Zones

Experts say it takes 21 days to change a habit.[84] 21 days of consistent, repetitive behaviour for it to set. If it's an addiction, it could take as long as 35 days or more. There is no quick fix to changing habits. Instead it means days practicing the future mentally with well-formed sights, sounds, sensations and intention that wire and fire new clusters of neurons, while allowing that those that do not serve the goal to atrophy.

By deliberate design we can move from same old, same old to a new normal. When we focus the mind, the emotions, and the image of what we want in detail, by planning a new reality inside our heads before it actually happens, we expand our bandwidth of tolerance. This happens by starting with the current self in the Change Cycle on page 115. With practice we reach a tipping point. Once that point has been reached, we are no longer satisfied with the current and shift into the future zone, which becomes the new current zone. We have overcome the chasm of uncertainty by creating a more compelling experience *inside our heads* by rewriting the software. This new and exciting state has been created using the way we imprint any new learning: with images, feelings and words.

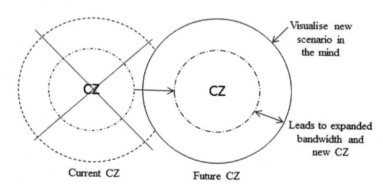

Visualise new scenario in the mind

Leads to expanded bandwidth and new CZ

Current CZ       Future CZ

**Creating a new CZ mentally which renders the old obsolete**

Once the new has become normalised, the old is relegated to the past and we have experienced a growth spurt. Unlike cold turkey or New Year resolutions, we actually have to condition/create the future in the present until the current becomes obsolete.

## Conditioning

One of the jobs of the subconscious is to maintain a state of ease together with a steady level of performance in the most economical way. Being fearful, tense, embarrassed or anxious (or numerous other states) very quickly pushes us to retreat when facing new challenges. Every CZ's mantra is 'No Risk'.

The subconscious uses its storehouse of experience as its guide. Whenever our senses alert us to an unusual or unfamiliar situation, it scans our emotional history, goes through a checklist of safe/unsafe, high risk/low risk, opportunity/threat associations in nanoseconds, and flags it as 'unknown', a 'risk', or 'opportunity'. When we return to the familiar, we are subjecting ourselves to what we have learned or been conditioned to see as normal.

In some parts of the world a baby elephant is trained at birth to be confined to a very small space. The mahout will tie its leg with a chain to a post planted deep in the ground. This confines the baby elephant to an area determined by the length of the rope. Though it will try to break free, the rope is too strong and it learns just how far it can go. Once the elephant has learned that it cannot go beyond a certain distance, it has been conditioned and no longer needs the chain.

Conditioning defines our reality; what we have learned and believe to be true - whether it is or not. How? By the beliefs, values and practices of our upbringing. Conditioning may be something unconsciously absorbed, something we were taught or something based on someone else's opinion, hardened through repetition into a *certainty*.

Once we understand what we have learned, how our 'training' has shaped us, how we were confined by a glass watering can or a length of rope, only then can we break free.

If change was easy we would all be exactly what we wanted to be. The words 'comfort zone' hold the key. People – you and me – are averse to change. We resist it, just as brushing our teeth with the other hand feels uncomfortable. Take the simple act of folding your arms across your chest. Try it, and notice which arm is placed over the other. Now cross them the other way and notice how you feel. We default to what feels comfortable, even though there is no pain, no spike of guilt, no question of right or wrong. We do it because it is what we do. Habits such as this just 'happen' and regulate our behaviour 95% of the time.[85]We grow up *believing* this or that information, often downloaded without awareness, and, like the elephant, become stuck with it.

Dr Joe Dispenza's sequence of drivers illustrates how we end up in a predictable State of Being. Thoughts, actions and feelings are recycled in predictable ways, where the same thoughts drive the same choices, actions and behaviours that lead to the same experiences and feelings, which drive our thoughts. Today will be the same as yesterday, the day before and tomorrow.

Our challenge is to break this loop to create something new. All learning and beliefs are second nature. Learning is a choice, a deliberate move to expand our horizons that makes the strange or scary less so, and the unfamiliar increasingly the new normal.

We all know how challenging change can be, even if it's perceived to be better than the present. Lotto winners, without notice or preparation, are thrown out of the familiarity of their lives. It's no surprise that nearly half of lottery winners are unable to adapt to their changed circumstances, and are broke within five years. Other studies show that lottery winners frequently become estranged from family and friends, and incur a greater incidence of depression, drug and alcohol abuse, divorce, and suicide – a high price to pay for something as seemingly inconsequential as restructuring one's comfort zones.[86]

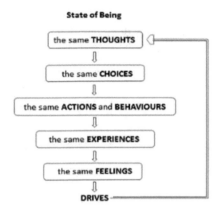

**State of Being**

from Dr Joe Dispenza, *You Are the Placebo,* Hay House (2014)

States of Being are also what scupper New Year Resolutions. Fed up with this or that behaviour or habit, we decide that *from tomorrow/ next week/ next year I am going to* . . . Our rational upstairs brain takes charge. We are resolute. Uncompromising in our decision. But sadly, by the end of January or March, we have reverted to our old ways – our downstairs brain and its emotional attachment to the familiar has overpowered our intentions. Willpower, logic and rationality have once more proven to be unreliable contenders in the contest for change.

## Common beliefs about Willpower

As someone wisely observed, we seem to have two personas, Bully and Willpower: the one who wants dessert and the one who wants a lean body, and tragically the Bully very often gets its way. Willpower isn't something we 'have', a commodity, like petrol in the tank that is available to us until it is used up. We might describe it as determination, drive, resolve or self control.

The key factor about trying to exercise willpower is we are using the wrong part of our brain. We might win the battle in the short-term, but before long we will have succumbed to the old patterns, those we learned using thoughts, emotions, images, sight, sounds, smells. All our senses came together to build the super highways that govern our behaviour. When we use only our reasoning - our thoughts and willpower – we are attempting to change an embodied belief with a disembodied alternative. What chance does that (albeit determined) 5% of our brain power have against the remaining 95%?

Our mission should be to augment our willpower with an image of what want using all our senses and faculties. In other words, we have to create a new reality, pump it up with colour, feelings, words and images *before* it actually happens. Installing this new software must replace the old with feelings of pride, joy and purpose by creating new neural pathways. Feeding the new and starving the old, and then rehearsed over and over is the only way the outdated will be replaced. It all goes back to where we begin in the Cycle of Change.

This method of visualisation allows it to overcome the Bully that is the speedier and more powerful emotional brain, evolved for our survival. Our habits govern 90% to 95% of our actions and over-rules the logical, reasoning part of the brain.[87] Putting all our eggs in the willpower basket on a whim sets us up for failure. The persuasive emotional brain steers us back to that place of homeostasis; tranquillity reigns when we revert to our usual hand when brushing our teeth. We have become the victims of Hebb's Law, superhighways of habit which the rational, thinking brain is impotent to change.

## Influence and Growth

Freeing up our 'stuckness' needs new ideas, habits or beliefs and then practicing them. Let's imagine we could take everything we know and place it in two concentric circles. One circle reflects the totality of what we can do something about, the things we have control over, and the other circle represents those things we cannot, such as the threat of war or government borrowing. These are represented as the Circle of Concern and Circle of Influence.[88]

Stephen Covey's Circle of Concern reflects those things we worry about. It is where our fears and impotence lie, our reactivity and over-whelm. It holds all the things we can do nothing about. When we spend our energy and resources in the Circle of Concern, our efforts achieve little and our wasted energy achieves nothing. We become impotent and reactive. Think of global pollution and we are a long way from serenity.

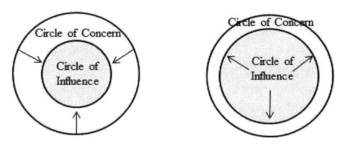

**from The Seven Habits of Highly Effective Families by Stephen R. Covey, Simon & Schuster 1997, with permission**

A more poetic parallel to this concept is St Francis's Serenity Prayer: 'God, grant me the serenity to accept the things I cannot change, the courage to change the things I can, and the wisdom to know the difference.'

The Circle of Influence represents the situations we can take charge of. It is the domain of courage, of our ability to learn and grow, and is the seat of confidence. Instead of being rendered feeble by global warming, it contains those aspects we are able to act on, like making choices to recycle to reduce our personal polluting footprint. To cycle instead of drive. When we direct our purpose to those things we can do something about, we expand our sense of control.

Faced with an issue, we can choose if it belongs in the Circle of Influence or Concern. The circle we choose is energised. If the situation is something we can take care of by stretching ourselves, we play bigger. It is well documented that successful people focus their energy on solutions rather than problems, expanding their proactivity and reducing those areas for which there is no payoff.

The opposite is true. If we invest our energy in the Circle of Concern, our impact is nil, our frustration escalates, and our sense of effectiveness is snuffed. Time and energy spent in the Circle of Concern is wasted.

The film, *The Shawshank Redemption* illustrates this concept through the story of a banker convicted of a double homicide. Andy Dufresne maintains his innocence and finds a way of surviving nineteen years of harsh prison life, while establishing a friendship with fellow convict "Red" Redding. Although the story is about friendship and hope, it reveals a great deal about both aspects of this chapter: the power of comfort zones and Circles of Concern or Influence.

In psychological terms, people incarcerated for a lengthy period undergo changes in social and life skills as a result of depressing and rule-bound environments: they become institutionalised. The effects of prison rule and rules imposed by inmates themselves, of having no autonomy, of being isolated from what was their 'normal', of having privacy and dignity stripped, alters their psychological and emotional resilience. Their comfort zones are changed and Circle of Influence shrinks. Indeed, the difficulty of returning to and integrating into civilian life after a lengthy incarceration has more than anecdotal backing.

Andy Dufresne skilfully negotiated the slippery slope of institutionalisation. Even at extreme personal cost he maintained his identity and created a vision for his future. His focus was on what he could do under the circumstances; where he alone could exert control. All his energies went into expanding his Circle of Influence with the concurrent shrinking of his Circle of Concern.

You will recall the Cycle of Change and Self-Talk Cycle from the previous chapter. These simple models demonstrate how we, alone, can begin to be the architects of our transformation.

With this in mind, I want to revisit the State of Being model referred to earlier. It illustrates how today's thoughts affect tomorrow and the day after. However, when thoughts change, we create new choices, actions and behaviours as they cascade down with new possibilities. Using this model to top and tail Andy Dufresne's story, his adaptation to life in prison required him to rise above being undermined and depersonalised. He had to think outside the box (new thoughts) and understand where best his influence lay (Circle of Control). He invested in himself. Taking the long view, he used his existing skills and developed new ones. He had a plan and laid the foundations one step at a time; he set himself up for success always with the end picture clearly visualised in his mind.

**NEW REALITY = New State of Being**

```
┌─────────────────────┐
│     new THOUGHTS     │◁════════════════╗
└─────────────────────┘                  ║
           ⇓                             ║
┌─────────────────────┐                  ║
│     New CHOICES      │                  ║
└─────────────────────┘                  ║
           ⇓                             ║
┌──────────────────────────────┐         ║
│  New ACTIONS and BEHAVIOURS   │         ║
└──────────────────────────────┘         ║
           ⇓                             ║
┌─────────────────────┐                  ║
│   New EXPERIENCES    │                  ║
└─────────────────────┘                  ║
           ⇓                             ║
┌─────────────────────┐                  ║
│    New FEELINGS      │                  ║
└─────────────────────┘                  ║
           ⇓                             ║
   DRIVES ─────────────────────────────────╝
```

**from Dr Joe Dispenza, *You Are the Placebo,* Hay House (2014)**

Reality is driven and created by our thoughts. What we think and the choices we make count. We are integrating left and right, upstairs and downstairs brains, conscious always of our ability to find the middle ground even as we stretch ourselves. This is how we impact our lives and those of our community. New thinking is what will empower each of us to continue to grow and expand our individual and collective influences,

# 11 Motivation

This chapter looks at the place of motivation and its contribution to our wellbeing. It begs the question why it is so difficult to improve our health, our relationships and wellbeing with their many benefits, when all it takes is a few simple adjustments to the way in which we conduct our lives. Motivation is the energy that propels us to act or behave in certain ways, even if the end result is something we might regret, (like eating an entire packet of biscuits just because it's there). What gets us up in the morning. Why we write shopping lists. What ensures we keep our mobile phone close to us every minute. Why we watch TV – and continue watching even when we know we should be doing something else.

Understanding motivation begs the question: Why we do this or that? The answer could be a *must*, or with a shrug *just because* ..., where the most comfortable action usually wins, even if it is not the most important or, indeed, in our best interests.

## Needs and Wants

Motivation can be internally or externally driven. According to various theories, motivation directs us to minimize pain and maximize pleasure, towards our goal or away from what we want to avoid. For purposes of economy of effort, we often take the line of least resistance. In other words we exercise choice: to move toward a goal, or provide as many reasons or sets of logic to avoid it – the classic *toward* or *away from* drive.

The motivation of all species is to survive and reproduce in spite of conditions that may not quite match their individual needs. Air, water, food and shelter are external primal motivators that occur across the animal kingdom. But it is the psychological, social and emotional needs, internal motivators of the human species, that give our lives meaning. This aspect of *meaning* is unique to homo sapiens. In his amazing book *Man's Search for Meaning*, Viktor Frankl identifies *meaning* as the single most powerful factor that allowed him and others to survive the Holocaust. Meaning is an internally driven motivator. Many of his fellow inmates who lacked a vision beyond incarceration perished days before liberation; without meaning they had lost their motivation.

We can think of essential requirements for life as existing on a 'needs continuum', which stretches from survival needs at one end (external) to spiritual needs (internal) at the other. These top-end, human-specific needs are not critical, but if neglected, can impair our sense of purpose.

A child who is chronically isolated, with only their survival needs being met, will not reach their potential compared with a peer whose needs for healthy socialisation and nurturing are met. Early isolation and neglect denies the child the opportunity to learn the rules of social engagement and/or acquire language, which can lead to later psychological dysfunction. A child thus deprived might lack the ability to communicate, be fearful of others or not understand social interaction. Social connection – esteem, belonging, safety – is not something humans want. It is a basic need.[89]

Spiritual needs, at the 'meaning' end of the continuum, are not those enshrined in religious dogma bound by rules and punishments, but rather the expression of higher-order values such as compassion, truth, selflessness and love – components of Frankl's 'meaning'. The more we stretch ourselves, realise and fulfil our talents and take responsibility for our purpose, the more we move toward transcendence.

When our social, emotional, psychological and spiritual needs are met, we flow into wellbeing and self-actualisation.

A want, on the other hand, is the desire to acquire something that is dispensable, driven by the demands of the emotional brain. Even our language confuses us, such as 'I need a new outfit for Mary's wedding'. A want is passing and shallower than a need. It is the expression of something we would like to have, but is never necessary to satisfy us at a soul level. A want has the power to lure us into believing our self-esteem or status will be enhanced once we possess it – an external prompt that temporarily fills an inner void. Many individuals are driven by the fallacy that meeting their wants will satisfy them: when I get (fill in the blank) I will feel ..., or when I have ... I will be ... The belief is that owning the latest gizmo will do the trick. It is the quick fix for a symptom, but fails to address the cause.

One only has to witness the media frenzy to know that, for example, the latest mobile phone's promise of greater storage capacity, sleeker design, faster camera, or longer battery life and other must-have advantages, will drive the consumer to replace the unit they own, even though their current model functions perfectly. The product may be seen by the owner as bestowing some sort of status, the acquisition of which, they believe, raises their status. Owning the latest/biggest/fastest brand name is a want in the guise of a need.

Instead, meeting and satisfying our needs is an introspective, more gratifying internal exercise. Meeting a need is achieved in increments towards a purpose rather than in reactive bursts of attention as brighter or lighter gadgets are dangled before us. Nor are needs limited to objects. We hear statements like, 'when we move', 'when I qualify' or 'when I lose weight', if-then thinking that suggests a void will be filled conditional upon something else happening, sometimes called wishful thinking. Wants are the territory of the downstairs brain, the search for a band-aid to fix unmet emotional, psychological and social needs. Wants engage parts of the brain, needs engage the whole brain requiring awareness, practice, effort and the acceptance of delayed gratification.

## Theories of Motivation

It is worth touching briefly on some of the theories on motivation.

Maslow's Hierarchy of Needs (1943) (Physiological, Safety, Love and Belonging, Esteem and Self-actualisation) is an early theory offering a staged level of needs from primary survival needs to self-fulfilment, self-actualisation and transcendence. In this theory, successive higher needs rely on the stability of the ones below it. An explanatory tale might best shine a light on this theory.

A professional man was well established in his career; with all levels up to his Transcendence needs being met. In looking both forward and back, he realised there was more to life than work, and dreamt of time out to give expression to his passion – excursions with his canvasses, paint and easel. He could smell the paint, feel the wind in his hair and the ball of excitement in his gut. Tragically, the tail end of a hurricane flooded his home rendering it unliveable, and in a flash his basic needs of security and safety were destroyed.

According to Maslow he could no longer feel the wind in his hair until such time as his home (his Physiological and Safety Needs) had been restored.

Tony Robbins, author and life coach, theorises six human needs as the template by which we unconsciously make decisions. Also represented as a hierarchy, he argues that we take action as a result of our needs, the order of which differs from person to person. He lists the six needs as: Certainty, Uncertainty, Significance, Connection, Growth and Contribution.

Let's also illustrate Robbins's model with a simple example. Patricia's primary need is for Certainty and Connection. She does is driven by her need to avoid or minimize the stress of the unknown, thriving on predictability and routine. Connection describes her need to belong, to love and be loved by others. She's a normal, everyday young woman who has been in her job for four years. She places great value in her team and department in the insurance company where she works. Having warm and functional relationships with her colleagues is key. She is offered a promotion that would require her to take exams, move location, liaise with external agencies and be more mobile. The promotion comes with a salary increase, and she could certainly do with the extra income.

She is pleased to have been recognized for promotion (Significance), but the alarm bells were ringing. The promotion would require high levels of responsiveness, initiative and creativity (Uncertainty) while engaging with unknown people, strangers, on a functional and factual level (moving office and the need for mobility, therefore losing the potential for Connection). In her model of the world, everything about the promotion cancelled out what she most valued about her present position, Certainty and Connection. After much consideration she declined the promotion and her colleagues thought she'd lost the plot. Even she was unsure of the exact reasons, but she knew in her gut it didn't feel right.

Peter's primary need is for Growth and Uncertainty and is married to Patricia. Growth prospers in the fertile ground of learning, new experiences and new challenges. Peter's second need is for Uncertainty, the drive for variety in order to relieve boredom, predictability and stagnation. His model of the world is quite different from his wife's.

He is frustrated at her decision to turn down the promotion, pointing out all the reasons why she should take it. She counters with all the reasons why she should decline. Neither understands the other's rationale, and their differences hang like a shroud over them for several days.

Robbins's theory of motivation has intuitive value, but is not clear quite how an individual discovers the order of their unique motivational imprint, let alone understand those of their partner.

A third exploration of motivation, which for me has greater intuitive value, is Human Givens[90] (HG). Identified as physical, emotional and spiritual needs, it has some parallels with Robbins' needs. When our mental and emotional resources align with our values, we are stable and enjoy good mental health. When one or more of our needs is out of balance or absent, optimal thriving is compromised.

Unlike Robbins's and Maslow's hierarchical models, the HG approach is represented as a wheel, where each segment is an equal and integral part of the whole. The metaphor of a wheel goes further to illustrate the need for balance, each part contributing to the robustness and function of the whole. For example, we all need a certain amount of attention, but an attention seeker can be the person we all try to avoid By the same token, if my idea of myself as someone who is always giving (and not receiving) attention, the balance is out and I end up feeling sidelined and, before long, almost certainly will feel resentful. Chronic unmet needs inevitably lead to emotional and physical challenges.

The HG wheel is scored according to its label from 0 to 10, where the centre scores 0 – no satisfaction at all, and the rim scores 10 – total satisfaction. The completed wheel is like a snapshot and provides a visual of where to begin goal-setting for change. The fullness and complexity of life cannot be caught (in the example given) in 8 segments, but it does offer flexibility.

This example of a completed wheel shows high and low scores. We might look at the three areas scoring lowest relative to the others: Security, Giving and Receiving Attention and Mind-body Connection.

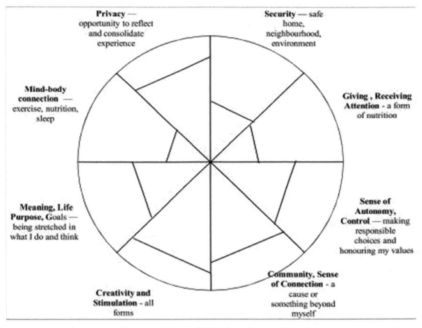

**Human Givens Wheel to Assess Needs**

Security needs can range from the more patent such as bullying in the workplace or at school, being threatened by a landlord about increasing the rent and thereby making the tenant vulnerable, or any other implied or subtle threatening behaviour that deprives the individual a sense of control. A less obvious case might be a migrant dispersed on a no-choice basis where they experience social and cultural isolation. Because Security will be interpreted differently depending on circumstances, the wheel gives individuals the opportunity to identify what particular aspect/s contribute to their low score, and what they need to do to raise it from, say, a 3 to a 5.

Giving and Receiving Attention might require a conversation with a trusted friend for feedback in how they perceive you in relation to your low score. If it was easy to identify our blind spots, we probably wouldn't have the problem in the first place. Do you talk too much or too little? Do you drive your own agenda at the expense of others, or give in and resort to silent resentment? An increase in score might be achieved by a decision to let two people speak before jumping in. Or to lower the volume. Or to just listen.

The Mind-body Connection could be educational, spiritual, cultural or social, or to steer their career in the direction they wish it to take. It could be to avoid contact with a particular person who undermines their sense of worth (external), or return to mindfulness practice (internal). Or it may be linked to nutritional decisions or the quiet, reflective time you do not take. Rather than trying to work out how to lose two stone, and giving up because of hopelessness and feeling like a failure (yet again), it is more helpful to ask what you need to do to bring your score from 4 to 6 — in other words, in manageable and realistic increments. Something simple like getting off the bus one stop earlier and walking the last ten minutes, even if it is raining, would contribute to the individual's sense of control.

Being aware of your wheelprint has the potential to expand your sense of self. The Wheel as a tool is also flexible. It can incorporate any label, such as Personal Space, Spirituality, Status, Career or Intimacy: the list is endless. In other words, the wheel above could have any number of substitute labels to reflect differing needs.

At this point you may well have concluded that using the Wheel is really an exercise in goal-setting with little to do with motivation. As mentioned earlier, motivation is the energy that drives our purpose.

And if a simple tool like the Wheel can direct our energy and give focus to our intent, then it has legitimacy.

Picking low-hanging fruit as a means of winning with minimal associated cost builds trust in your ability to set and achieve small goals. Banking your successes in this way builds muscle memory, and can be achieved in multiple areas across the Wheel simultaneously. Small but regular wins are like the enriching concept of compound interest which help grow confidence, and is an investment in yourself.

## Inherent Resources

Nature has blessed us with the resources necessary to meet our needs.[91] We might doubt it, believing instead that others are better equipped or more talented than we are. Trust, instead, that our inherent resources lie dormant rather than are absent. Like a seedling, everyone has resources that will flourish given the right amount of water, light and LTC.

We may be overly focused on *WHAT we should think* rather than the far greater impact of learning *HOW to think*. Just as we can build muscle through resistance training, so should we begin to exercise and build resilience and growth through conscious development of the resources nature has endowed us with.

We all have resources of **emotion** and **instinct** that serve us in our will to survive. Our inner senses constantly give us feedback if only we learned to listen. Instead of ignoring the messages our bodies give us, begin to trust them. For example you really want to refuse a request, because your body is loud-hailing 'No!', but instead you give a rictus smile and say something like, 'Certainly I will – it's no problem'. Disregarding emotional instincts comes at a huge personal price. Resentment is toxic, and is a long, long way from wellbeing. A good rule of thumb is not to make important decisions when angry, in a hurry, frustrated, tired or any other negative state of mind. Buy time, if necessary, by saying you will get back to them. Begin to recognise and trust the messages your gut is giving you.

- **Empathy** is the ability to understand and build rapport with others. It is a key element of emotional intelligence, the link between self and others, because it is how individuals understand what others are experiencing. It's the ability to recognise someone else's pain as a witness, but not get caught up in their drama. It's about being open-hearted and fair-minded. So instead of jumping to conclusions or judgment, step into the other person's shoes and guess what might be going on for them.

- **Memory** allows us to recall experiences and learn from them. Let's benefit from the miracle of our minds because success and failure leave trails, which, too often, we overlook. Remember the Learning Cycle in chapter 9? Missed opportunities to learn from mistakes guarantees we remain stuck. Take responsibility. Take charge of learning from experience and have fun with feedback; get smart on how to make it work.

- Freeing up the **imagination** allows us to problem solve creatively by trying out ideas mentally first. It also provides the potential to be proactive instead of reactive – and is tied in with tracking what worked and what didn't from memory. Every invention first starts in the imagination – isn't that astonishing? Imagination is not fired when we are in our comfort zone. Being comfortable snuffs imagination. 'Necessity being the mother of invention' can provide limitless ways to solve problems, some more practical than others. A valve or shunt to release water pressure from the brain of a child born with hydrocephalus was invented by the father of the child, an engineer, not by a doctor. From the mindset of curiosity, asking *if there were a solution, what would or could it be?* can inspire miracle solutions.

- **Intuition** is closely related to instinct, giving us understanding without the need for conscious reasoning. It is about perceiving and interpreting the world through subtle or unconscious mental processes. Women being more attuned to nonverbal cues is explained as an evolutionary advantage to better decode the needs of children and potential mates. But there are many men skilled at reading others' emotions. Let's stop generalising about intuition and start taking responsibility for ourselves one day, one experience at a time.

- **Reason** is the conscious, rational mind checking emotions, analysing, planning, fine tuning, evaluating. Unfortunately it goes into hiding when agitation or anger intervene. As with emotions and instincts, defer any decision until you're in a calmer, whole-brain state of mind.

- The **observer self** is the part that has the facility to press the pause button, step back, be objective and recognise itself. Do we buy the latest phone to feel (momentarily) like a trail blazer or to feel important? Is it confidence we're after? Or a sense of worth? Or being the leader of the pack? Let the observer self instead become aware of what *need* it is trying to satisfy. Once the emotional brain has been reined in and the true reason for purchasing the gizmo has been identified, only then is it possible to plot a new path or expand our circle of influence.

  The critical action here is to pause. To connect with the aspect of your brain that is shouting loudest – left, right, downstairs? Discover which aspect is being the bully. Take time to gather the information you need to balance the decision you are about to make. Is the rational *you* being coerced by your four-year old having a tantrum?

Exercising a fragmented brain denies the observer self: we lose the ability to overrule the default operating system. When we become aware what is driving our actions or thoughts, we have taken a big leap in understanding our personal, motivating engine, and started engaging all parts of the brain. Pause. Question what lies behind the object or goal you desire. Ramp up the resources of your whole brain. Give it space and enough time to show how smart it is. Give it the vocabulary to identify the desire behind the *want*; the urgent voice of the unfulfilled inner child. Be patient. Support the observer self to take stock to understand what is really behind the decision. Whole-brain attention and taking responsibility will result in a different outcome. A whole-brain approach silences the critic and allows us to ask what we need to do differently, and where we need to direct our attention. A quote by Henry Ford would seem appropriate here: 'Coming together is a beginning; keeping together is progress; working together is success.' Each of us has the tools. Let's explore our personal drivers to succeed, one step, one experience, one new awareness at a time.

# 12 Reality

This chapter examines what happens when our focus is fixed on one thing at the expense of another – and what this tells us about the 'true' nature of perception. It explains how we 'see' things not with our eyes (or other senses), but rather as interpretations by the brain. Anomalous as this may sound, it's true. We will look at the filters in place and how they fool us into believing our 'truths'.

The senses, under bombardment from the environment during waking hours, are not switched off during sleep. Stimuli in the form of heat, light, taste, smell, sound and pressure are all forms of **energy** that we allow in or filter out, depending on their significance. For example, a mother will waken to the cry of her baby while the father does not. Unless, of course, the mother is not there, in which case he will. Why does he not waken the first time? Because at a subconscious level he knows she will.

Even awake we may not be aware of something until our attention is drawn to it. Take the clothes you're wearing. In contact with probably more than 70% of your body, you are hardly aware of your jeans or your footwear until the belt is too tight or the hot spot on your heel draws your attention. It's not because clothes are light in weight – who hasn't felt their face brushed by a spider web? It's not the presence of something, but that our attention has locked onto whatever is significant, making it difficult to ignore.

Can we be conscious and unconscious at the same time? It sounds like a trick question, but let me ask: how many of us have arrived at a destination, not quite remembering the details of the drive? We stopped at the lights, turned corners, avoided cyclists and collisions. Our senses allowed the information in, and the brain then automatically interpreted and executed the action of driving. Much of our lives – up to 95% it is said[92] - is conducted in this state of conscious unconsciousness, on automatic pilot. Which raises the question of how?

We have blind spots associated with all of our senses. Whether a physical, mental or emotional distraction, it is our focus and our conditioning that lets in or blocks out information. In broad terms we create a reality by focusing on what we want or don't want in our lives or, in the case of the hot spot on your heel, by selectively paying attention to one thing at the expense of another. Energy is energy and is neutral; it goes where we direct our attention. Universally applicable, we may not choose to be fearful or anxious, but when attention is constantly on those aspects of life we want to avoid, we focus on potential threats and lose out on serenity.

A short practical example of energy flows where attention goes is given in the sentence below. Read it once.

> Geoffrey and Frances of Findlater Street in Smithfield were free to think of nothing but their holiday until clouds of ash forced flights to be diverted and cancelled.

Now read it again and count the number of times the letter *f* occurs.

Did you find more than eight? Or nine? Count the letter Fs again. There are eleven.

We may wonder why or how we missed a few Fs. Could it be that we pronounce *of* as 'ov', or that the word is small and insignificant? Whatever the reason, this exercise reminds us that we don't see with our eyes but with our brain. The things we miss are called mental blind spots, and we all have them.

## Interpreting stimuli

Our worldview is based on how we perceive an event and make sense of it using story or drama based on associations with our past, sometimes referred to as pattern-matching. Recognising patterns is a process whereby information from one experience is matched with information from another. This ability allows us to understand clusters of information coherently and economically, to recognise that an oak or apple tree are both trees/ For most, pattern matching generalises a fear of snakes to all snakes, whether venomous or not. Based on context, history and exposure, pattern-matching allows economy of mental effort from direct or indirect experience, as well as from the experiences observed in, or passed on by, others.

Have you ever met a person out of their usual context, only to discover that you cannot quite place them/their name/where they fit in? In other words we use a host of memorised cues and associations, emotions and context to draw conclusions. The complex processes of remembering, categorising, comparing, measuring, interpreting, adapting, contextualising and understanding all contribute to the *sense* we make of things.

We all know people who have experienced or witnessed the same event but interpreted it differently. Who hasn't been promised a wonderful film or book, only to be disappointed? A painful divorce for one may be a release for another. The loss of a job may open the door to a more creative or fulfilling career. It all depends on the context, the associations with which we match events and the filters we use to create our reality. Reality, then, is a relative construct and is relevant to how we show up in our lives.

E + R = O reminds us it is not the event or stimulus itself, but how we interpret it that shapes our experience. Use that moment's pause well. Be deliberate. Change from hard to soft focus, switch from a green to red filter, and what we perceive is changed.

When we lock on to an idea or habit, our zone of focus is narrow and blocks out distracting information. Locking on can be good – but, again, its value is relative to circumstances. If a golfer had a million euro resting on a five metre putt, it would be advantageous for her to lock on and cut out the buzz of the crowd and a mobile phone that should have been switched off. If we missed a few Fs along the way, what else might we be missing? What unknowns are passing us by?

A quote by Donald Rumsfeld conveys the complexity of reality: 'There are known knowns, the things we know that we know. There are known unknowns. That is to say, there are things that we know we don't know. But there are also unknown unknowns. There are things we don't know we don't know.' The known knowns are 'facts' which, we've established, are often the opinions or truths that have been passed on to us – remember 'flat-world' thinking? Our challenge is to keep an open mind about everything.

## Confirmation Bias and the Lock-on/Lock-out Principle

It's common for us to fall foul of another well-known psychological trap, that of confirmation bias. This is where we opt to interpret fresh information in a way that endorses ideas on which we are already fixed. It describes how we actively seek out and assign weight to evidence that confirms a belief or hypothesis, while ignoring information or evidence that challenges it.

In my own case, for example, I don't think I have ever heard a positive statement made about George W. Bush or Donald Trump. Not because there weren't any, but rather that my personal filter would have allowed in only information that supported my narrow opinion of both presidents.

Closer to home, confirmation bias or the lock-on/lock-out principle was never more evident than in Ireland's own Kerry Babies case. Two dead babies were found in Kerry in the spring of 1984. The first was a baby boy with multiple stab wounds found on Cahirciveen beach. The second was a baby boy buried on the family farm of Joanne Hayes, the person accused of both murders.

Joanne Hayes, a single parent, had sought medical help for a full-term miscarried birth. A Garda investigation to trace the mother of the first (Cahirciveen) baby led to Joanne. In spite of haematological evidence stating that the baby could not have been either hers or that of her boyfriend Jeremiah Locke, the prosecution came up with a complex theory attempting to prove the two babies were twins by different fathers. So strong was the need for detectives to believe their own story, that they discounted a range of medical, marine, tidal and psychiatric evidence, and instead clung to their hypothesis that Joanne Hayes had murdered both babies. Having locked onto Joanne as the murderer, the investigating team was unable to separate what was deemed by specialists to be two unconnected cases. The State has recently apologised to Joanne for this miscarriage of justice. However, the record shows how 'reality' can be interpreted, depending on who is most strongly invested in the outcome.

## Groupthink

'Groupthink' means that the desire for an outcome is driven by the group's agenda that might go something like: if you're not with us, you're against us. Groupthink members have an illusion of invulnerability and make decisions based on collective rationalisation. Believing in the inherent morality of the goal, group pressure interferes with critical evaluation. Even a group member's desire to present an alternative view is covertly silenced perhaps because they fear being ridiculed or humiliated.[93] Groupthink, a concept by social psychologist Janis (1972), generally results in unchallenged, poor-quality decision-making, as in the case just mentioned.[94]

Other indicators of groupthink are the illusion of unanimity, discounting warnings, and wanting a quick-fix. When members believe their own version of events, they ignore the ethical or moral consequences of their decisions. Dissenters are under pressure not to express arguments against the group's views, and self-censorship rules. History can provide no end of examples, such as Hitler or Robert Mugabe.

Groupthink leads to botched jobs, the incomplete exploration of alternatives, failure to examine risks, poor or biased information gathering and selective processing, a failure to have a Plan B and, given all of the above, a very low probability of success. An individual who challenges the group culture would be courageous and would almost certainly be ostracised.

Putting two and two together, anyone can see how the dynamics of groupthink, confirmation bias and the lock on/lock out principle can be applied to ourselves and our self-talk. It is as if we have more than one voice inside our heads, and are cowed by the one that bullies us the most. We are reminded not to make fools of ourselves, to keep our heads down, not to stand out from the crowd. It is the voices of the different parts of our brain and mind, fragmented and fighting for dominance, that lead us to make unsound, poorly-thought-through decisions. The intention of the subconscious mind is to protect us from the dangers of humiliation, being singled out, being shown up as cowards – scripted and stored for self-preservation because of our history. Being conscious of the complex filters in place, we can learn to recognise the dominant voice, acknowledge its intention in that space before R in the E + R = O equation, and give ourselves a moment to examine alternatives or act before we fall victim to the unwanted habit.

## Reframing

Reframing is the ability to see an existing situation from a fresh viewpoint. A woman I worked with became choked up when she recounted how her mother, who was chronically ill, would frequently keep her from school to do bedside or household chores. She had three siblings, but was always the one singled out to help. Sadly, she fell behind at school, not surprisingly had little confidence in her academic ability, and became a Department of Education statistic as an early school leaver. The unproductive world view she had formed in her early years was that her mother favoured her siblings. She had locked onto the belief that she wasn't good enough – a belief she had rationalised as a child to make sense of her circumstances.

Through reframing, she was able to step back and appraise the situation differently. As an adult she knew that her mother would not deliberately have disadvantaged her – that perhaps her mother had called on her because of her dependability. This process of cognitive reframing altered the woman's worldview as surely as if someone had flicked a switch. It frequently takes a third party, an objective eye or hearing the same information presented with a different slant, for an individual to have this type of *aha!* moment. It illustrates how one very small shift can sometimes make an incalculable difference. Words by Einstein remind us that 'problems are not solved by the logic or reason that created them in the first place'.

Whether the example is that of an adult holding on to her small-child thinking or a team of adult professionals convinced of a particular 'truth', the power of the concepts of lock-on/lock-out and groupthink should never be underestimated. We are all victims of our thoughts to varying degrees, leading us to invent extraordinary inter-pretations of 'the facts'. Irrespective of which reality filer holds sway, we have it in our power to make a switch once we are aware of the power dynamics working to protect us from ourselves. That is the na-ture of *reality*. Little wonder that it is so difficult to extricate ourselves from the webs we have woven.

# 13 Science and Mind

This chapter looks at how discoveries by biologists, neuroscientists and others are laying new foundations for understanding the mind. New awareness is providing a revised framework for how we can consciously influence the connections that make up body/mind/spirit.[95]

## Genetic Determinism

In the mid-1800s, Sir Francis Galton and his cousin Charles Darwin were key proponents of the theory of biological determinism, claiming that most human characteristics, physical and mental, are determined at conception by hereditary factors.

In the nineteenth century, at around the same time as Darwin and Galton, Louis Pasteur, who founded the science of microbiology, proved that germs cause disease. He invented the process of with pasteurisation and contributed to developing the earliest vaccines. His work set in motion the idea that infectious diseases were the result of external agents acting on the cell. He was right, and much has been achieved in the wake of his discoveries.

A contemporary supporter of Pasteur's line of research, Claude Bernard claimed, 'The stability of the internal environment [the *milieu intérieur*] is the condition for a free and independent life'[96], suggesting that the robustness or health of the cell's environment **determines its future**. The *milieu intérieur,* the *nurture* aspect in the nature vs nurture debate, is the result of the mind-body axis constantly changing and influencing the cell's response.

In 1953 Watson and Crick discovered the three-dimensional double helix of DNA and promoted its role in determining our genetic heritage. Certain now of DNA's role as *the* genetic determinant, research shifted focus away from environmental influences. Biological science focussed on individual human behaviour and disease characteristics being controlled by our inherited genetic make-up. (Galton had previously established the eugenics movement: the 'science' of improving the human race through selective breeding or genetic engineering.) According to the theory of genetic determinism, our destiny is programmed: our genes call the shots, and we have no more control over them than we have over eye colour or height. In the nature-nurture debate, nature won hands down; genetic determinism ruled.

Doctors are trained to fulfil the role of diagnostician and to facilitate management and treatment. The practice of disease specialities grew out of the need for more targeted health care. Practitioners vary, but many now use a broad 'bio–psycho–social model' of diagnosis.[97] Psychological, spiritual, lifestyle and nutritional factors combine to play a role in illness and healing, evident from the experiences of people who have recovered from cancer and other diseases.

My partner was diagnosed with a lymphatic tumour that was inoperable due to its location in the V of two major arteries. Going cold turkey, she went on a 7-day organic green juice fast, followed by a concerted organic, high-alkaline, no-sugar, no-alcohol diet along with a mindset that focused on health, not disease. She exited a highly stressful job, undertook gentle but consistent aerobic exercise, and started paying attention to what her body needed. At a consultation with her oncologist, she asked if the PET scan she was scheduled to have in a few weeks would show any shrinkage of the tumour. 'What would make it do that?' was his reply. In the absence of any intervention other than those she had put in place herself, the report following her PET scan three months after diagnosis, stated: No evidence of disease. She had created the optimal environment that enabled her body to heal itself. The oncologist was pleased to give her the news, but showed no interest in learning what she had done to bring about this result.

What caused the tumour to disappear cannot be scientifically proven because it was not possible to exclude the influence of confounding variables. But the steps she took to optimise her body's own defense systems and attending to her *milieu intérieur* significantly altered her health trajectory.

Much progress came about as a result of the Human Genome Project (HGP) that covered a thirteen-year programme which began in October 1990.[98] The HGP was an international collaborative programme whose goal was the complete mapping and understanding of all the genes of human beings – the human genome. In June 2000 the HGP announced that it had assembled a working draft of the sequence of the human genome - our genetic blueprint. This major milestone involved two tasks: placing large fragments of DNA in the proper order to cover all of the human chromosomes, and determining the DNA sequence of these fragments.[99]

This deeper knowledge led to developments in ways to treat, prevent or even cure thousands of diseases that afflict mankind.[100] Loathe to use the word 'cure', many physicians use 'in remission' or 'no evidence of disease' instead. In remission means that tests, physical examinations and scans show that all signs of the disease are gone. They also use 'partial remission', meaning the patient can take a break from treatment as long as the disease remains inactive.

In cases where no medical, surgical or pharmaceutical intervention has taken place, being 'in remission' indicates that something profound has occurred in the body by the body through its innate potential to heal itself. Being in remission supports the notion, sometimes controversial within more orthodox circles, that the body has the ability rewrite the rules of disease and even hereditary diseases by addressing health with a paradigmatic shift in diagnosis and treatment. This is not science fiction, but is based on results within and across multiple health disciplines.[101]

Scientists and researchers are proving over and over again that we are not subject to biological determinism, presumed after discovering DNA, but instead are active participants in who we are and who we can become.[102] The HGP General Director is quoted as saying the HGP Report is like a 'a manual, with an incredibly detailed blueprint for building every human cell. And it's a transformative textbook of medicine, with insights that will give health care providers immense new powers to treat, prevent and cure disease.'[103]

## Epigenetics

*Epi* is from the Greek word describing 'on, upon, above, in addition to'. Put together, epigenetics is the study of genes and their behaviour as a result of chemical changes occurring outside of the cell – in a petri dish, tissue or organ – in which the cell or community of cells finds itself.[104]

Since HGP the emergence of epigenetics has quietly but steadfastly taken place. As a young graduate cloning stem cells from cultures in petri dishes, Bruce Lipton's professor told him that if any were ailing, to look first to the cell's environment, not to the cell itself, for the cause. What he discovered was that cells thrived when provided with a healthy environment. When the environment was less than optimal, cells faltered. Cells presented with a nutritious substance moved toward it with the equivalent of open arms and those presented with a toxic substance retreated,[105] demonstrating that individual cells can move selectively. When the environment for failing cells was upgraded, cells quickly recovered. Bernard's theory of 100 years previously also recovered.

Lipton and others have proven that it is not DNA that determines how or what genes will be expressed, but the messages coming from outside the gene – from the environment it inhabits. For our purposes, the quality of the environment is created by the smorgasbord of our thoughts, emotions, nutrition, lifestyle and beliefs. Hormones in keeping with our state of mind are constantly being produced. Stress hormones, for example, flood the body in just the same way that the environment influences genes in laboratory petri dishes. If they are not spent through flight or fight, they directly impact the way the gene expresses itself. According to epigenetics, how we show up or rate our achievements can no longer be attributed to our genetic inheritance, but instead is governed by the mindset based on our interpretation of events.[106]

Not limited to physical symptoms, epigenetics spans temperament as well. We are not born hot-tempered or intolerant, but have learned to be – and thus believe ourselves to be – short in these qualities. Epigenetics argues that it is habits that press our buttons rather than DNA. When cells are faced with a constant chemical signal of, for example, over-vigilance, they will eventually adapt to that environment, so that even when neurotransmitters of calm are present, they default to that to which they are habituated. That is why it can be so hard to break the habit, in this case, of hypervigilance. With the right support and awareness and by changing the filter on matters that cause interference, we can bring about change.

What science is telling us is that if we control the controllables, for example environment, lifestyle, diet and level awareness, we upgrade our *milieu intérieur*. In spite of the many curved balls we are thrown, there are ways we can exercise choice. To ensure healthy and sustainable living we can be selective about what we place within or leave out of our Circle of Influence. When we become aware of the constant and negative drip-feed of self-talk, horrific revelations via the media of injustice, pollution or disaster, we need to notice where we are focusing our attention. Step out of the Circle of Concern and into the Circle of Influence.

The factors to manage are those generated in the body itself — feelings, thoughts and expectations, and those from the environment, such as pollution, nutrition and things that cause stress. Maybe we could get up half an hour earlier to beat the traffic or simply switch off the TV. Based on our perceptions, we will behave like the cell in the petri dish and move *toward* or *away from* the stimulus or event. Once we are in control and can see clear water beyond our habits, once we realise we can change tack and circumvent the storm, we have started to take charge of our growth and our wellbeing.

## Becoming our own agent for change

I grew up believing that the aim of science was to prove things. I was wrong. One of its aims is to disprove them. Let me give you the example I learned at university.

If we start out with the hypothesis that *all swans are white* — and a hypothesis is a proposed explanation for a phenomenon — continuing to find white swans does not prove or disprove this hypothesis. It merely adds to the belief that already exists, even if it is wrong. All it took was for Australia to be discovered and for one black swan to be found, and in an instant, the belief collapsed.

This *swan* theory applies to science as well as to our beliefs and habits. All we have to do is find one piece of evidence to disprove it, and use it to question or rewrite the script that no longer serves us. Much of the time we ignore the contradictory evidence or, perhaps, consider it luck. Instead, we need to grasp the contradiction as something of value.

When we recall an event, our literal brain experiences that one event as many times as we replay it. Rehearsing the scene again and again ensures we're well-practised. Think weeds, grow weeds. Think negativity, grow negativity – or conversely, optimism or joy or positivity.

A whole-brain approach is the starting point. Dr Rick Hanson, a neuroscientist and practicing Buddhist, provides a simple story[107] from his own experience, summarised below.

As a nerdy kid, and later as a nerdy teen, Hanson ended up with lots of confused and unpleasant feelings inside. Mostly he felt bullied or put down, with only a few good things happening in his life.

When he went to college, he became conscious of a few small wins – someone paying him a compliment or smiling at him. He felt good for a moment, and then got on with whatever he was doing. When he dismissed or ignored the good feelings, they quickly dimmed, and he reverted to feeling disempowered.

What he discovered was that if he spent 15 or 20 seconds thinking about the positive experience and letting the feelings sink in, he felt different and better. The more he connected with the good feelings, the more confident he grew – the good accumulated and the negative reduced.

**Reproduced with permission from Dr Rick Hanson, from**
***Hardwiring Happiness*, TEDx Marin, 2013**

Hanson became aware that dwelling on the good was changing his brain, and his brain was changing his mind. Without practice there was no remembering. Effectively, there was stasis. Any good thing that happened had no lasting value *unless it was downloaded with conscious attention*. In other words, passing through our successes too quickly should carry a health warning. Instead, dwell on the good. Savour the feelings. Wire and fire them so that, as Hanson says, 'passing mental states, given attention, become lasting neural traits'. His take away from this is: practice the feeling and the memory, and soon new connections will be installed. If we can follow his advice, we benefit from our triumphs, no matter how small.

# 14 Healthcare under the Microscope

This chapter explores further how we can consciously and purposefully participate in our own wellbeing.

## Personal Healthcare and Quantum Physics

Quantum physics is the branch of science that provides an explanation for the nature and behaviour of matter and energy at atomic and subatomic levels. But what on earth does quantum physics have to do with health and wellbeing?

All animals are a collection of organs, tissue and bone made up of cells. What are cells made up of? Molecules. What are molecules made up of? Atoms. What are atoms made up of? Protons, electrons and other even smaller particles. What are protons, electrons and sub-atomic particles made up of? Energy.[108] Even though it would seem we are solid, nothing could be further from the truth. Instead we are gazillions of atoms flying around in energy fields that vibrate and oscillate in pattern frequencies.

Indeed, if we extend beyond the animal kingdom to the universe, quantum scientists have demonstrated that the earth, moon, sun and distant galaxies are made up of the same particles and vibrating patterns, the resonant frequencies which are comparable to sound in the world of music.[109] A practical example might be where an inanimate object, such as a musical instrument, will generate enough energy when a string is plucked to impact the same string on a guitar on the other side of the room. The sympathetic vibration in the string of the second, passive guitar is what science calls harmonic resonance, where like resonates with like.[110] Like resonating with like is the quantum explanation.

We are energetic bodies that vibrate and oscillate, sending out vibrations as thoughts, intentions and behaviour. Every thought and body response to emotion, cognition, behaviour and health sends electrical signals that can be measured using specialised equipment, biofeedback, polygraph and electroencephalogram (EEG) technology being familiar examples.

## From incoherence to coherence

The tune-up of an orchestra in the pit is disordered. The oboeist gives an A, which is followed by all the stringed instruments tuning to A. Each then tunes the remaining strings relative to A. For anyone who hasn't experienced an orchestral tune up, the sound is chaotic.

The conductor raising his baton produces a different experience, his leadership ensuring that the sounds become clear and purposeful, coordinated and flowing. With proper management and direction, members of the orchestra have moved from the individual to a part of the co-ordinated whole, have transformed from incoherence to coherence.

Cell output is similar. Cells working according to their individual needs are intent on their own purpose, whereas the conductor bringing focus and coordination to the bigger picture creates harmony. With the conductor in charge, (that is you and me), each section communicates optimally with the others.

Incoherence = Disease or dysfunction

### Coherence = Health
From Dr Joe Dispenza, Coherent and incoherent energy frequencies,
*You are the Placebo, p 194* with permission

From a quantum perspective, coherent frequencies create health, and incoherent frequencies cause disease or dysfunction. Higher, coherent frequencies are generated during, for example, meditation, prayer or gratitude, while anger or stress produce lower, denser and more incoherent frequencies.[111]

A body in balance – incorporating all aspects of wellbeing – is resilient, energetic and self-regulating. Balanced energies regulate the body's chemistry and hormones. Practices such as mindfulness, meditation and guided imagery are proven to reduce stress and anxiety, performance inhibitors long identified as impacting attention, attendance at work and other factors affecting the bottom line.[112]

Cells require focus and vision to avoid the incoherence and dysfunction that can occur if they're left to range freely,[113] because negative messages or those lacking control hijack coherence. Coherence comes from clarity of thought, purpose, coordinating disparate parts and bigger-picture intention. When the brain and nervous system are tuned into higher frequencies, all the parts – molecules, hormones, cells – are synchronised and bring fuller functioning to the body. This is epigenetics in action when the conductor is in charge.

The conductor working from a script directs the harmony and blending of disparate parts. In the same way, a healthy body and mind, rewarding job and loving relationships all call for a strong and matching vision/script to control the output. Being mindful of our thoughts and self-talk, using feedback and trusting the gut all contribute to wellbeing. Without the score as a guide, a conductor would be unable to reveal the magnificence of Debussy, Rachmaninoff or Chopin. When our personal values and actions are in sync, we experience the expression of flow and harmony.

## Curing and Healing

Before going further I wish to bring your attention to what I see as the difference between curing and healing, words often used interchangeably. A *cure* (bearing in mind the reference earlier to cure vs remission) can happen without healing, and healing can happen without a cure. Training in medical schools focuses on curing. Curing means *eliminating evidence of disease*, while healing means *becoming whole*.

Healing is an internal process of body, mind and spirit, something we actively participate in to create the *milieu intérieur* that will enable the body's inherent defences to correct the imbalance. It requires our active participation to look at root causes: being compassionate towards ourselves, managing stress, improving lifestyle and dietary choices, and rooting out toxic relationships to optimise the body's healing potential. It is about eliminating excess, being moderate in all things, being aware of boundaries, increasing assertiveness, expressing gratitude and being forgiving– many of the points discussed in this book.

Multiple individual stories like Chris Wark, who beat stage 3 colon cancer using diet, and other accounts from his collection of survivor stories,[114]or Dr Terry Wahls's *How I Went From Wheelchair To Walking By Changing My Diet,* are testimony to how individuals overcame extreme health conditions in spite of or in lieu of their medical intervention history.[115]There is nothing spontaneous about spontaneous remission or healing. A lot of hard work goes into the changes needed to bring about a return to health. Nor is there a one-size-fits-all solution. These people, and others' stories too numerous to mention, testify to changes individuals introduced that contributed to their recovery. Under-standing the significance of factors within their control directed their actions to restore themselves to health.

## Complementary approaches

Healing and energy flow use techniques from time-honoured traditions of mind-body interventions such as acupuncture, yoga, kinesiology, ayurvedic medicine, homeopathy, meditation, tai chi and Neuro-Linguistic Programming (NLP). Balance and harmony can be non-invasively restored and maintained within the body's energy system by tapping, massaging, pinching, calming, movement or touch that connect energy points on and within the body. Reiki traces or swirls the hand over the body along specific energy pathways to un-block or balance flow. Yoga and tai chi use exercise or posture designed for specific energetic effects. Manual therapies use massage and deep tissue manipulation, or movement prompts, such as Rolfing. Muscle testing evaluates the body's imbalances and assesses energy blockages, functioning of organs, nutritional deficiencies and food intolerances. These, and many other energy medicine interventions have withstood the test of time and, in many cases, are being acknowledged as having value by some orthodox healthcare practitioners.[116]

Visualisation or guided imagery generates sensory-rich images of behaviours or events we would like to have happen in the future – our goals. While not a first-line treatment for serious diseases (or any condition), it nevertheless is a free and effective form of intervention. The schema of what one desires is practiced over and over in the mind, using imagery, colour, exaggeration or symbols with the appro-priate emotion to forge new neural pathways. Dr Carl Simonton[117] of the Simonton Cancer Center in the USA, describes how the patient chooses their own imagery. It might be an emoji gobbling up a cancer tumour, or blasting the same tumour into smithereens with a laser, or enveloping it in a colourful hot air balloon and releasing it.[118] Guided imagery combines pictures and feelings that befit the goal of wiring and firing neuronal connections in the brain. His main thrust is two-fold: increase the positives and eliminate the negatives.

Guided imagery has shown that both physical and psychological reactions in certain situations can be improved.[119] Repeated imagery can build experience and confidence in both the patient's or athlete's ability to improve under pressure, or in any configuration of possible situations. It is where the individual exercises control to overcome anxiety and limiting beliefs, increases confidence and generally takes charge of the numerous variables to improve their situation – much like the conductor in our orchestra. Visualising a positive scenario or outcome using words, pictures and feelings, in the full knowledge that body and mind do not differentiate whether the image is real or imagined: the practice promotes the appropriate emotional, physiological and neuronal responses.

The majority of mainstream health practitioners do not see any conflict in augmenting mainstream with complementary treatments, particularly when they have used such interventions themselves .[120]However, GPs are trained to use a linear model to diagnose and treat patients. The model suggests that if there is a problem, the source lies in one of the steps between A and Z. If a machine is not working and is diagnosed with a faulty gear, it makes sense to fix or replace the gear. Once the faulty gear at C is corrected, the assumption is that D and E onwards will re-engage and once more function properly. Many people's experience and expectation of healthcare is that conditions termed *disease* are treated with medication or surgery using this near-universal A → Z, cause-and-effect rationale. Patients seeking healthcare most often select this as their first line of treatment.

Holistic and complementary practices, on the other hand, generally adopt a body-mind approach in the quest for optimising health and wellness. Integrative or holistic interventions (functional, osteopathic, chiropractic, naturopathic, homeopathic, integrative and acupuncture practitioners) are specialists who regard health and wellbeing as interdependent parts of the whole, where one part being out of balance will affect the whole.

A holistic healthcare model is one of balance and flow, where interactive and cross-referencing body systems, emotions and beliefs communicate using feedback, feed-forward and cross-communication.[121]

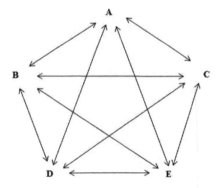

**Diagnosis and Information Flow in Holistic Health Management**

Unlike the linear A → Z model of health care, the diagram A to E shows how applying a diagnosis to C would not make sense by isolating it from the whole. Tissue or joints accumulating negative energy would almost certainly show up as aches and pains or disease. But instead of masking the condition with a painkiller or specialised drug, a holistic practitioner would try to determine the cause and the factors contributing to the problem: body alignment, diet, repetitive strain, tension, stress retention, mind-set, coping strategies, lifestyle. Joint pain or arthritis would be regarded as a symptom of something out of balance, rather than a diagnosis requiring drug or other treatment.

## Personal Participation in our Wellbeing

At the time of writing, I had a blood test diagnosing an underactive thyroid. The prognosis was to go on to thyroid medication for the rest of my life. No way did I want to subject my body to a long-term chemical regime when there was the possibility of diagnosing and correcting imbalances naturally, even though the medication route is the treatment choice of the majority of patients and doctors.

Taking a leaf out of my own book, I took charge of my choices. I researched extensively and used a buckshot, rather than a bullet approach. I cut out gluten, reduced sugar intake, increased supplements of omega-3, Vitamins C, D and E, sprinkled kale and turmeric powders on food and in smoothies, and made every effort to clock up 10,000 steps per day. I investigated essential oil blends and applied them topically to my thyroid area.[122] Blood tests 4 months later reflected the changes:

- No need for thyroid medication
- Decrease in bad cholesterol
- Weight loss (without dieting)
- Moved away from pre-diabetic status

The good news is that *all* metrics improved between my first and second blood tests 4 months apart. Motivation came from my very clear goal to avoid thyroid medication; every difficult decision point, of which there were many, was made easier. I wasn't exercising willpower Instead my goal and very strong desire was not to take medication for the rest of my life. Lifestyle changes and Internet research led me to augment some things and drop others to optimise my body's ability to restore itself. I subsequently attended a naturopath who supported my healing journey, a managed GI tract and liver cleanse, herbal medicines and advice on supplements. A follow-up blood test has shown continued all-round improvement, and highlighted aspects for specific further treatment.

# 15 The Energy Body

*In every culture and in every medical tradition before ours, healing was accomplished by moving energy.*
**Nobel Laureate in Medicine Albert Szent-Györgyi, MD (1937)**

This chapter expands on the notion that we are bodies of energy whose every molecule produces a resonating electrical frequency that can be measured. Dr James Oschman is a scientist, cellular biologist and physiologist who has provided us with an elegant theory of the human body and how it is impacted by energy medicine, despite this being dismissed by some in conventional medicine.[123]

Energy medicine and energy psychology are travelling companions. However, evidence is mounting that energy psychology techniques are significant and powerful tools for both self-help and clinical treatment, as demonstrated by the growing body of proponents, practitioners and those benefiting from its numerous interventions.

## Components of Energy Psychology

Thought, emotion, sensation, and behaviour join forces to create the body-mind connection. The body-mind link is driven by our energy systems which include **meridians, chakras** and the bio- or electro-magnetic field, also called the **aura**.

As most of us know, meridians are energy channels whose origins in ancient traditions were stimulated to release and prevent congestion. Needle insertions along meridians in acupuncture can and have been substituted using other methods such as heat, electricity, magnets and lasers.[124] (Tapping as a method of palpating meridians is covered more extensively in chapters 16 and 17.) Meridians connect the surface of the body with the internal organs, and when too much or too little energy flows, dysfunction or disease can result.

Seven major chakras or energy centres (chakra in Sanskrit means *wheel*) are associated with the body via the endocrine system. They run up the centre of the body like an electric power line, connecting meridians that function in much the same way as electrical wiring in a house. Each chakra has its own frequency, and keeping them in balance is essential in order for us to function properly. When our chakra frequencies are in harmony, we feel connected to ourselves and with others. When under- or over energised, we become 'out of tune' and vulnerable to minor incidents or major upsets. [125]

The aura exists beyond the body in seven energetic layers, each layer relating to a chakra. The layers represent the physical, mental, emotional and spiritual conditions that interpenetrate each other to work as a complete system. Closest to the body is the emotional field, followed by mental and spiritual vibrations, connected to the chakras. The higher the vibration, the further from the body it lies. Though not visible to the majority of people with the naked eye, Kirlian photography shows the existence of energy fields in all living matter. When part of a leaf is missing, for example, the aura of the original whole leaf's outline remains.[126] (The visible aura, in many artists' impressions, is the halo in pictures of Jesus and other saintly characters.)

Atoms and molecules vibrating in patterns respond to the messages they receive from the environment and from our thoughts. We are all walking, talking masses of resonating energy. Indeed, the placebo effect referred to in earlier chapters is an elegant example of the mind-body connection being led by intention or expectation. Recalling the Circle of Influence, it is something within our control.

## Heart Energy

Almost certainly your biology lessons at school, like mine, taught that the heart is a muscle with four chambers that pumps blood throughout the body. Yet recent discoveries confirm that the heart is far more than this. Unlike the brain, it can be serviced and replaced, but, up to recently, has been seen as a servant to the brain.[127]

Discoveries have now confirmed that the heart is far more than a pump. The HeartMath Institute (www.heartmath.org) reveals that the heart and brain work together in harmony. The new field of neuro-cardiology has evidence that the heart has its own 'brain' in the form of specialized neurons called sensory neurites. This 'heart brain' is similar to the network of neurons found in the brain, but can act independently of the brain to think, learn, remember and sense our inner and outer worlds.[128]

Confirmation of the independence of the heart brain comes from recipients of heart transplant surgery through the phenomenon of *memory transference*. (As many as 200 heart transplants are carried out on adults in the UK each year and 2004 were carried out in the EU in 2013-14.)[129] [130] Memory transference ranges from preferences for specific foods, dreams, memories, as well as shifts in personality. It even led to the arrest and conviction of a murderer whose victim's heart was transplanted into a child who was able to provide police with detailed evidence of the crime, including the name of the perpetrator.[131]

The heart as the most powerful source of electromagnetic energy in the human body produces the largest rhythmic electromagnetic field of any of the body's organs.[132] Because of its power, it is important that we bring our heart brain into coherence whenever possible.

A quote from authors of The Living Energy Universe, Gary Schwartz and Linda Russek, suggest that, 'If the 20th century has been the Century of the Brain ... then the 21ˢᵗ century should be the Century of the Heart'. Indeed, ancient traditions, the Old and New Testaments and indigenous cultures, all in slightly different ways, urge us to seek the wisdom of, and ask questions of, the heart and then sit quietly and await answers from it.

Biofeedback equipment provides visual evidence of the body's energy expression. This technology enables the individual to exercise real-time control over behaviours such as breathing and heart rate using relaxation or other energy psychology techniques. Relaxation methods aid the management of conditions such as stress, chronic pain, anxiety or high blood pressure.

You will remember that healthy cells vibrate at high frequencies. When stress or disease are present, the lower frequencies were likened to the cacophonous sound of an orchestra tuning up, rendering cells unable to communicate with one another. Coherence relates to the quality of the signal and heart-brain coherence is directly linked to the quality of emotion we feel. [133]

We can improve our wellbeing in a two-step heart brain coherence exercise from the HeartMath website called the *Quick Coherence Technique*, as follows:

### Step 1: Heart-Focussed Breathing

Focus attention in the area of the heart. Imagine your breath is flowing in and out of your heart or chest area. Breath a little slower and deeper than usual.

### Step 2: Active a Positive Feeling

Make a sincerer attempt to experience a regenerative feeling such as appreciation, care or love for someone or something in your life.

While outside the realm of the body's energy systems, an analogy with the laser beam exemplifies the power of coherence. Each colour in the light spectrum has a different wavelength. For example, blue light has a shorter wavelength than red. A laser beam is different, as it is an artificially created light beam that does not occur in nature. However, scientists figured out a way to produce a narrow beam of light in which all of the wavelengths travel together in phase, or coherently. Laser beams, being very narrow and bright, concentrate their light onto a tiny spot. Having multiple and varied uses, laser precision tools can cut through diamonds or thick metal.[134] The power of coherence – in this case light – speaks for itself.

Achieving and maintaining a coherent and resilient energy flow requires self-management of all our resources: physical, emotional, mental and spiritual. In other words, the whole brain ensuring our needs are met and in balance lead to wellbeing. Physical resilience is a measure of the flexibility, strength and health of the body. Emotional resilience is the ability to self-regulate, maintain a positive outlook, embrace emotional adaptability and seek supportive relationships. Mental resilience is the ability to sustain focus and attention, and the capacity for mental flexibility. Spiritual resilience is a commitment to core values, trusting your gut, embracing tolerance, contributing to community and being non-judgmental.

## What Drives Energy?

In my training classes I get participants to hold a paper clip on a length of thread over a sheet of paper showing N-S-W-E compass points. Resting an elbow on the table with the pendulum dangling above the compass, they are instructed to say North/South in their heads. Before long everyone's pendulum is swinging North/South. Then East/West. Then round and round. It works – at least with 99% of participants. Comments made are, 'Am I psychic?' or 'This is scary!'

Neither psychic nor scary, it is nothing more than energy expressed and manifest by words and intention. Energy is a property of the universe. But it is also a property of our thoughts. Energy, which we have learned attracts its likeness, moves the pendulum north-south in harmonic resonance.

It is this matching of frequencies, the harmonic resonance touched on earlier with the example that allows us to locate our car in a busy car park without setting off all the others when we activate our key. What is being demonstrated in quantum terms is that a vibration in one object can trigger another on the same frequency at a distance, because energy travelling through space connects with its equivalent. It means frequencies are discrete and tune in to others on the same wave band.

The downside of vibratory resonance is the effect of our negative thoughts, which also emit vibrations. When we replay a bad experience (that happened once) multiple times, our body experiences it again and again with equal doses of detrimental and cumulative stressful hormones delivered with each replay. The mind, being literal, does not distinguish between what is real or imagined, but epigenetically resonates according to the messages it receives. So when I tell myself what an idiot I've been, or will I ever get my act together, I am replaying that resonance and punishing myself with unhealthy consequences using thought alone.

Whether by gravity, light, sound, smell, taste, touch or heat – each experience we encounter is an exchange of energy. Energy is energy and neutral; it only becomes positive or negative when we interpret its value relative to ourselves, our worth, our values. When we speak, acquire learning, communicate or take action we are expressing ourselves as energy beings. We always have the choice to have it build us up or put us down.

Events leave imprints in our bodies, especially when we experience big T or small t trauma. Who hasn't experienced a spasm in the stomach when asked to stand up and address a public meeting. This reaction has been generated spontaneously by our stomach for reasons of self-preservation. Most of the time spikes of emotional intensity are spent without consequence. However, when there is no resolution to significant or cumulative emotional events, hormones are hoarded like arterial plaque, hardening and blocking energy flow until there is a crisis.

Researchers have worked to locate the source of blocked memories. What they discovered is that the filing system for memories can occur in any organ, gland, muscle or bone in the body.[135]We may have blanked, blocked or dissociated from a memory, but the body does not have the capacity to forget, until or unless the negative emotion can be adequately processed and released. If not spent, trapped emotional energy can accumulate and cause physical ailments.[136]

Not related to blocked memories, but nevertheless of interest in this chapter, was BBC2's documentary covering the topic of phantom limb pain.[137] Phantom limb is a painful sensation that is perceived within a body part that no longer exists. No treatment for phantom limb pain has yet been successful, including drugs, anti-epileptic medication, and analgesics.[138]

With his patients unable to afford drug treatment, an Indian doctor, Ramachandran (1996), came up with the idea of using a mirror to reflect an image of the existing limb. The treatment is the patient observing the sound limb in a mirror. When scrunching toes on the sound limb and seeing the reflected image moving, the mind interprets it as if the phantom limb is moving. The results of this artificial visual feedback of mirror therapy are significant.

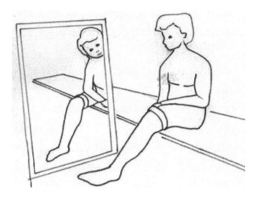

**Mirror Therapy for Phantom Limb**

British war veterans, astounded at the results of mirror therapy after years of traditional pharmacological therapy, reported their relief when appearing on the BBC programme. Here was evidence of how re-wiring neurons provided pain relief to their non-existent limb. Using the simple technology of a mirror was not only something over which they had control, but the more they practiced, the greater the effect. Instead of dulling the pain with drugs and having to deal with side effects, participants were actively rewiring the brain's architecture. In energy psychology terms, mirror therapy delivered a visual message to cells and this changed the amputee's experience. Pain was alleviated with lasting results.

The takeaway from this chapter is that to boost energy flow and facilitate our healing and wellbeing we can use energy in the form of visual cues, needles, heat, colour, vibration, deep breathing, mindful attention, heart consciousness and heart coherence to promote a sense of control and wellbeing.

# 16 Emotional Freedom Technique

People are curious about Emotional Freedom Techniques (EFT) or Tapping, and surprised or dismissive in equal measure regarding results attributed to its practice. This chapter will look at its origins in the ancient art of Chinese acupuncture, which few question, and how the practice of Tapping or EFT has a growing cohort of champions because of the results.

## Background

Acupuncture used in Traditional Chinese Medicine (TCM) has been practiced for centuries. Acupuncture and acupressure (manual pressure using fingers, elbows or feet) stimulate the meridians to connect and unite the energy flow through that point.

Emotional wellbeing is regarded as an integral part of health in TCM, where the major organs are associated with specific emotions. Feelings of joy and sadness, anger and calm are normal. It is when an emotion becomes stuck through excess, repression, being inappropriately expressed or turned inward, that TCM recognises it is no longer in balance and, therefore, becomes a cause for concern.

In other words, mental or physical imbalances are regarded and treated as *symptoms* of blocked energy or dysfunction in an otherwise healthy body. When emotions are not appropriately expressed, they become stuck and energy flow stagnates. Stagnation causes disease, and releasing blockages brings back energy flow. The belief is that once balance is restored to the system, the body, given the correct balance of nutrition, rest and exercise, can return to its natural state of healthy functioning.

A TCM practitioner educates the patient on the causes of their imbalance. The patient is encouraged to slow down, practice mindfulness or Tai Chi, conscious breathing or meditation, and to augment these with diet and nutritional supplements. Lifestyle and stress reduction are also key factors to be incorporated. Compared to the passive role of the patient in Western medicine, the TCM patient plays an active role in their recovery and ongoing health management.

It is at the crossroads of TCM and psychology that tapping has found its place by stimulating the energy system of the meridians at specific junctions while at the same time using target phrases that address the issues. It is the synergism of tapping and talking that merges East and West, body and mind, physical and emotional. It is non-invasive, specific, and has no side effects – distinct advantages in healing and health management. Tapping can be self-administered or used with the guidance of a trained practitioner. A number of peer- reviewed studies of tapping have shown it to be as effective as acupuncture. Indeed, Davd Feinstein, PhD suggests that it might be a more flexible intervention, as the sequence of tapping can be done by the individual themself as and when needed, with the phrasing updated to reflect the changing experience of the individual. Acupuncture and tapping do not remove the thought or erase the memory, but remove the emotional charge associated with the event.[139]

Feinstein is a clinical psychologist who has served on the faculties of The John Hopkins University School of Medicine, Antioch College, and the California School of Professional Psychology. In an interview he gives an explanation of the science behind tapping.[140] The amygdala are two almond-shaped areas in the brain responsible for emotions, survival, instinct and memory. When we are startled, arousal in the amygdala triggers the fight, flight or freeze response. Functional magnetic resonance imaging (fMRI) measures brain activity by detecting changes associated with blood flow. When an area of the brain is in use, blood flow to that region increases. Studies have shown that acupuncture was more effective than medication both in war veterans and Chinese people suffering PTSD due to earthquake trauma.[141] Acupuncture and tapping decrease arousal in the amygdala.

As mentioned in Chapter 6 (Anger and Trauma), we experience the physiological effects of fight, flight or freeze every time there is a real or perceived threat. Everyday living delivers multiple low-grade stressors in response to which it is not necessary to flee, fight or freeze. We may even consider the few small stressful events in any day are *nothing much,* but our autonomic nervous system will have downloaded the chemical messengers and these accumulate if not burnt off through practices such as breath-work, meditation, physical activity or tapping[142] .This build-up of stress hormones over days, weeks and months can leave us feeling fragile, burnt out or experiencing other symptoms like fatigue. Levels of unspent frustration or anger compound – who hasn't heard of road rage or 'the last straw'?

Studies have found that tapping lowered cortisol significantly more than other interventions tested, and correlated with declines in anxiety, depression and other psychological symptoms measured by standard psychological assessment tools.[143] How liberating to be able to deliver an effective treatment that promises no side effects.

Tapping came about through the work of Roger Callahan, a practicing psychologist and cognitive behaviour therapist in the USA in the 1970s. He had studied Applied Kinesiology or muscle testing, a method of diagnosis and treatment based on the belief that various muscles are linked to particular organs and glands. He also studied Chinese acupuncture.[144]

Callahan had been working for a year or more with Mary, a patient who had such an overwhelming water phobia that she could not bathe her own children. Although he had tried every anxiety reduction technique at his disposal, including suggestion, clinical hypnosis, biofeedback and more, nothing seemed to work. He felt discouraged. One day while they were in session, Mary complained about a feeling in the pit of her stomach whenever she thought about water. Callahan knew that an acupuncture point located beneath the eye was directly linked to the stomach meridian.

He asked her to tap below her eye, hoping it might balance a possible disturbance in her meridian energy system and thereby lessen her stomach symptoms. He had no idea that it would have profound implications for the future of what has become known as 'energy psychology', or the mind-body connection.[145] Mary tapped under her eyes and the unexpected happened. Instead of experiencing relief from her stomach symptoms, she called out in surprise that her fear of water had gone. Callahan didn't take this seriously until she jumped up and ran toward the swimming pool in the grounds.

He decided to explore the possibility of using acupressure on certain meridian points to treat other patients with phobias. While not all responded to the tapping procedure as rapidly as Mary had, this experience marked an important opening up of the field of energy psychology. Callahan's technique became known as Thought Field Therapy (TFT). With TFT the client thinks of the problem while tapping the specific meridian points and monitors the emotional intensity using a scale of measurement from 0 to 10.

A student of Callahan, Gary Craig, simplified the 670 meridian points or windows where energy enters or exits the body.[146] He determined that tapping a strict order of meridian points was unnecessary, and instead developed one sequence that addressed all the organ endpoints no matter what the issue. The revised TFT was called Emotional Freedom Techniques or EFT.

EFT, regarded by some as pseudoscience, has nevertheless gathered momentum from observable results and patient self-reports, as well as from the growing numbers using it. The act of tapping interferes with the fire alarm wiring to the amygdala. It interrupts the flow of emotions associated with events while the individual simultaneously repeats phrases of self-acceptance, the combination of which deflates the bad memory, and the grip of trauma dissolves.[147]

Pain is pain, but addressing the emotional content of pain has been proven to reduce physical symptoms by lowering cortisol levels and calming the brain's fire alarm system.[148] In *The Tapping Solution*, author Nick Ortner provides a case study which gives Patricia's story, reproduced with permission. Having been in a boating accident, her L1 lumbar vertebra was shattered. Surgeons had stabilised her spine with four titanium rods and eight sets of screws and bolts. But the pain was excruciating, managed with morphine and a host of medication. In addition, Patricia had trouble sleeping, so sleeping tablets were added to her health management regime. She felt stressed and was exhausted from the pain.

Over the course of an EFT intensive weekend, she and her one-to-one course facilitator addressed everything the specialists had told her about her back – the diagnosis and prognosis – identifying all the beliefs she held about her condition. What she'd been told by the experts was that she would always have pain, that she'd never be active again, that her passion – yoga – was a thing of the past. The doctors' pronouncements locked Patricia into a mindset of victim. Until she tapped.

Tapping systematically, they addressed all the negative emotions her body had stored. By the end of the weekend Patricia felt no pain. The heaviness from the rods and screws in her back had disappeared. She felt hope for the future and focused on what she could do rather than what she couldn't. Soon afterwards she stopped all pain and sleeping medications and returned to yoga.

Evidence of the efficacy of tapping from empirical studies, case studies such as Mary's and EEG measurements are showing significant results. Sufferers of post-traumatic stress, motor accident victims, war veterans and phobics, among others, support tapping as a verifiable intervention.[149] Long-term and follow-up studies using EFT in war veterans reported no return of symptoms six months after receiving six one-hour sessions of tapping.[150]

Dr. Lori Leyden, Founder of Create Global Healing and Project Light, set up a non-profit organisation dedicated to trauma healing and heart-centered leadership for orphan genocide survivors in Rwanda using EFT, with remarkable results[151]. Traumatised by ethnic cleansing and the breakdown of the country's social, economic and systemic structures, hope and a future were non-existent for the majority of survivors. Project Light stepped in. It selected a cohort of young people to be trained as leaders and trainers in EFT. They, in turn, would deliver training for the benefit of others as well as use it in their own healing. Remarkable stories have emerged in this bottom-up, vision-led project. In a heart-warming turnaround, young people from Rwanda, via video link, helped in healing victims of the 2012 Sandy Hook Elementary School shooting in Newtown, Connecticut, (which also happens to be Ortner's home town). Miracles can and have happened.

Much information on EFT is available online. YouTube hosts numerous cases of healing in people who have experienced physical violence, rape, bullying and PTSD. Practitioner styles vary, as individuals experiment with variations on the EFT theme, but the end results demonstrate that there are many ways to tap out negativity and tap in health. Since my own introduction to EFT through brother and sister

Nick and Jessica Ortner, I have discovered Jenny Johnston and others whose outcomes speak for themselves. The results they achieve are nothing short of astounding. But remember, as with everything in life, along with the good, may follow the bad and the ugly.

## Buyer Beware

Before going any further, it is necessary to point out some of the arguments made against EFT. While EFT is a tool which can create breakthroughs in emotional understanding, suppressing these emotions in the first instance was an unconscious mechanism to survive. Unwrapping past trauma, alone or with a practitioner who has little regard for the safety of the client, could cause the individual to be overwhelmed by re-experiencing the trauma. Specific protocols to manage such situations are used to ensure the client's safe passage throughout the process.

Further, when a system teaches us that everything we experience is the result of something we created for our own survival, we may be burdened with feelings of guilt, shame or despair. We may resort to behaviours that might exacerbate the condition, or undermine the ethical and professional obligations of the practitioner to keep us safe. It is the responsibility of the practitioner to deal appropriately with such issues and to ensure the client understands the truth of their role.

Further arguments against EFT are that while it cannot do any damage directly, it may offer false hope and thereby delay patients seeking mainstream treatment regimes. Time spent on tapping could be time wasted. Again, there are protocols and guidelines to steer the client in the appropriate direction, pointing out that EFT and other interventions are not either/or, but can be this *and* that.

It is important to keep these caveats in mind. However, from my experience and from reading and viewing third party personal accounts, it would appear there are few conditions not responsive to tapping. Individuals suffering hypervigilance, chronic pain, antisocial behaviour, violent outbursts, poor self-image, substance abuse, nightmares and intrusive thoughts have had their lives turned around. At a 90-day follow-up with PTSD sufferers, the results fluctuated for one veteran in specific symptoms with reductions between 50% and 90%. At a different veteran's 90-day follow-up, symptoms of suicidal thoughts, paranoia, fear of heights, anxiety and fear of crowds had been 100% cleared.[152] It is unscientific to generalise from individual case studies, but it is the number of individuals who have experienced positive outcomes that gives credence to the benefits of tapping. Tapping unblocks the trauma of a UDIN memory (Unexpected, Dramatic, Isolating, No strategy - see page 77) via the parasympathetic nervous system by allowing it to be expressed, resolved and integrated.

I have tapped on myself to overcome procrastination, writer's block or frustration and overwhelm. I have worked with others who have identified ways of overcoming obstacles at work, dealing with relationship problems, childhood abandonment, rape, migraine, speaking in public, childhood sexual abuse, grief, lower back pain and numerous other blockages that prevent lives from flowing. I have witnessed astonishing successes and partial successes. In my learning curve as a practitioner, the miracle one-session cure may resolve an issue, but rarely do our challenges come individually wrapped. One of the benefits, though, is that individuals can tap on themselves at home or where- and whenever situations arise. This form of self-management is unlimited, free and with the potential to bring about immeasurable results.

EFT can be integrated with other methods such as drawing to help individuals express themselves or gain insight. A combination of symbolic drawing and tapping or metaphor engages the non-linear thought process, unlocking us from the logical, regulated left brain. This connects us with our subconscious, adding valuable detail and insight from an otherwise difficult-to-access world.

One client with whom I have tapped with over multiple sessions, wrote:

'Hazel created an environment where I felt safe – I trusted her implicitly. With her gentle probing as a coach, along with EFT, I was able to speak what I thought to be the unspeakable.

Within the recent past I had settled for a life of mere existence, I had turned my back on life because I did not want to be here. We tapped through tension in my face, panic, sadness, regret and more. The upshot was – I now know that I want to live, that choices are mine, and that it's ok to be exactly who I am right now. For me tapping has brought me to a place where I don't have to be so hard on myself. I have been reacquainted with a world of peace and love. I am now in a place where I feel that I have something to contribute to society and that EFT is a tool that I can call on in moments of overwhelm. So when the old feelings start to stir I simply and discreetly tap and soothe them until they are gone. The impact of all this on my life is more than any of us will ever know.'

Now if that isn't a testament to the power of tapping, then I promise to eat my hat.

Knowing about EFT or tapping is one thing, but doing something about it, as with other suggestions in this book, requires application. The next chapter is a guide to tapping; a step-by-step breakdown of the process that you may like to try for yourself. Even skeptics have been surprised at results in tapping away headaches, back pain or fear of public speaking. Go on, give it a try.

# 17 Getting Down to Tapping

Tapping works by pairing the memory/symptom/event/limiting belief/emotion with a statement of self-acceptance. This pairing uses two well-researched psychological techniques called exposure (remembering or naming an issue) and cognitive restructuring (such as reframing, all-or-nothing thinking, over-generalisation).[153]

Physically pulsating with the fingertips on the acupressure points on your face and body allows the brain's stress machinery to disengage. Once the conditioned association of the memory with the stress response is broken, it usually stays broken, thus bringing relief or substantially reducing whatever was causing the discomfort. Patricia's story in the previous chapter demonstrates this.

EFT is easy to learn, simple to apply and is safe. People have asked when they should stop tapping. Unlike prescribed medication, tapping delivers no negative side effects. Use it as and when it is needed. Use it before or after an event. Use it daily and join the many subscribers who do. Or, if you have stopped tapping and the condition returns, simply start tapping again.

The majority of tapping points are bi-lateral, meaning they occur on both sides of the body. It is not necessary to tap both sides, though we can if it feels right. We can tap with either hand. If we skip a point or forget, it doesn't appear to matter. Indeed, I came across one practitioner online who taps only on the karate chop point. There are 'Third Eye', finger, wrist and other points – but the illustration below shows those most frequently used.

If you are at a meeting and feeling stressed, you can tap discreetly on your inside wrist, karate chop or at the base of each fingernail –

the fingertip points (not shown in the diagram). Conscious of your stress, and therefore acknowledging it at some level, all you are doing is tapping without setup or reminder statements. Tapping in this way also yields benefits.

## Tapping Points

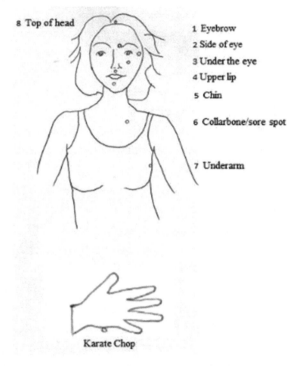

8 Top of head

1 Eyebrow
2 Side of eye
3 Under the eye
4 Upper lip
5 Chin

6 Collarbone/sore spot

7 Underarm

Karate Chop

When I started tapping on myself and before I underwent training, I had read about it, watched videos on YouTube and listened to hours of podcasts, yet was still uncertain where to begin or what to say. Lindsay Kenny (lifecoachingwithlindsay.com) provides a model where the constituent parts of a tree represent aspects that provide a starting point. The tree is merely a visual aid, where the leaves represent *symptoms* or side effects, the branches represent *emotions*, the trunk *specific events* and the roots represent *limiting beliefs*.

## Tapping Tree

| | |
|---|---|
| *Leaves* = | weight issues, self-sabotage, |
| S y m p t o m s / Side Effects: | addiction, pains and illness, clutter, procrastination, PTSD, ailments, sleeplessness |
| *Branches* = | fear, remorse, |
| Emotions: | disappointment, sadness, rejection, anger, stress, powerlessness, anxiety, guilt |
| *Trunk* = | car or other accident, |
| Events: | bullying, dysfunctional parents, abuse, punishment, criticism, injustice, being betrayed, abandonment |
| *Roots* = | I can't do anything right, I'm |
| Limiting Beliefs: | ugly, I'm not worthy, I'm not good at . . ., I've two left feet |

Let's say you have a headache. Looking at the tapping tree, you might think of it as a symptom of something else unknown at this point. So you begin by tapping on your headache. In other words, you start tapping with whatever is the most pressing issue. There is no ONE starting point; you can begin with a symptom, a side effect such as sleeplessness, an emotion such as frustration, a specific event such as tripping and breaking your arm or a limiting belief such as *I'm really hopeless at sticking to my plans.* You could even tap on, *I feel so unsure about this tapping - I just don't know where to start.* No harm can be done by 'getting it wrong' because there is *no wrong way.* Tapping is the interplay of feelings and talking, feelings and talking. Any new insight or awareness that arises is information to be used to further understand what's going on.

Tap on the most pressing issue – the pain in your back, the irritation you feel after the row with your partner, something you wish you hadn't done or the fact that you're such a procrastinator.

## How to Start Tapping

Don't fret - just talk about what's bothering you and tap. Remembering that there is no 'wrong' way, let's begin the process with whatever is the most pressing matter for you. Sit upright with both feet flat on the floor, and follow the steps:

1. Choose what it is you want to tap on – the problem or issue, which we use as a Reminder Phrase through the tapping sequence.

2. Create your set-up statement.

3. Score the level of discomfort between 1 and 10, where 10 is extreme and 1 hardly anything at all.

4. Write it down.

5. Start tapping.

## 1 Choosing what to tap on

The more specific you can be in describing your symptom or feelings, the better. In this way we can begin DIY healing.

Let's say you have a pain. Ask yourself the following questions:

Where exactly is it? Does it have a shape, density, colour or texture, is it hot or cold?

If the pain had an emotion, what would that be? Anger? Frustration? Helplessness?

Examining the pain or emotion, and locating where in your body you feel it helps to isolate it. One interesting observation, as you tap, is how the pain can change and shift around, or change in character. Be clear and specific about the adjectives you use – 'this light, sharp pain' or 'it's like a black cloud all over'. Just connect with it and then describe what you are feeling in a make-believe or metaphorical way.

Even before taking the first step, you might choose to add some powerful heart energy by placing a hand over your heart and breathing deeply and slowly three times with a positive intention such as 'I want to let go of this sharp pain in my lower back'.

## 2 Set-up Statement and Reminder Phrase

The set-up statement combines the issue or challenge you wish to tap on with a statement of self-acceptance. Beginning with *Even though I ... (*fill in the blank with whatever issue you want to address – the Reminder Phrase), and pair it with acknowledging yourself in a way that feels comfortable, such as 'I accept myself and [the issue] with love' or 'I'm just fine the way I am'.

> *Even though* I HAVE THIS SHARP PAIN IN MY LOWER BACK, *I accept myself with love* or, if that feels OTT, *I am willing to accept myself with love*

191

or

*Even though* I'M SO DISAPPOINTED IN MYSELF FOR EATING THE ENTIRE PACKET OF BISCUITS, *I'm fine just the way I am*

People often say they try to be positive, and that it doesn't feel right to dwell on the negative by repeating how disappointed they are. The purpose of the set-up phrase is twofold:

a) To name the problem

b) To accept ourselves despite the presence of the problem

Saying what we feel acknowledges our current reality, rather than ignoring it. Denial is a coping mechanism that gives us time to adjust to distressing situations — but staying in denial is counter-productive. Not accepting ourselves warts and all keeps us stuck. Our feelings of disappointment or anger do not go away when we deny them, when we pretend all is well with the world. Instead they pile up until they show up in another outburst or binge, leaving us further convinced of our inadequacies. Denial locks us into one small working area of our brain. Acknowledging and tapping lets us discover what lies behind our issue. When we finally acknowledge that we accept ourselves, we release the energy block and give ourselves permission to seek more empowering patterns. By releasing the pressure required to keep our shadow side hidden, we free up our brain to integrate its disparate parts, allowing whole-brain functioning to serve us as it should.

The purpose of the reminder phrase is to maintain focus on the problem while we tap to realign the energy disruption.

## 3 Scoring

Score the intensity of discomfort out of 10, where 0 is no discomfort and 10 is excruciating. Write it down, because we can easily forget how excruciating the discomfort was.

## 4 Start Tapping – Overview

Repeat the setup statement three times while tapping the Karate Chop point – that soft, cushiony muscle on the side of your hand. EVEN THOUGH I HAVE THIS PAIN IN MY LOWER BACK, I ACCEPT MYSELF COMPLETELY.

Starting with the eyebrow point and finishing at the crown point, tap lightly through each point five or six times in succession while repeating the reminder phrase – THIS SHARP PAIN IN MY LOWER BACK. Tap five to six times lightly and rhythmically on each point, repeating what it is you're feeling: THIS PAIN IN MY LOWER BACK or I'M SO DISAPPOINTED IN MYSELF FOR EATING THE ENTIRE PACKET OF BISCUITS. Tap two or three rounds using the reminder phrase, and add any other feelings or thoughts that may have sprung to mind, such as I'M SO ANGRY AT MYSELF AGAIN – YOU'D THINK I'D LEARN.

After each round, take a deep breath and check in if whatever you were feeling has changed – has it moved to a different part of your body? Changed in character or intensity? Or has a layer been peeled back and you've become aware of something new?

Introduce new phrases if something has come up. Tap through as many rounds as necessary to reduce your level of discomfort to 1 or 2.

**Score**

Give what you are now feeling a score out of 10 and write it down. After each round of tapping, pause and assess the intensity of the score, which may change up or down. If a new feeling or awareness arises, include whatever it is or change your reminder phrase. Matching what you say with any changes taking place is how to progress the tapping process.

| | |
|---|---|
| Karate chop: | 'Even though I am so fed up with myself for eating an entire packet of biscuits, I accept myself just the way I am' x 3 times |
| Eyebrow: | 'This feeling of anger and disappointment' |
| Side of Eye: | 'This overwhelming feeling of how pathetic I am' |
| Under Eye: | 'I feel it everywhere in my body and I hate the feeling' |
| Under Nose: | 'This feeling of disappointment in myself' |
| Under Mouth: | 'This 10 out of 10 feeling of disappointment and anger' |
| Collarbone: | 'It's unbearable. I feel such a failure' |
| Under Arm: | 'This unbearable disappointment and being such a failure for eating a whole packet of biscuits' |
| Top of Head: | 'I'm so disappointed with myself' |
| Score: | Deep breath, hands on heart, score out of 10 |

## Developing the Process

Let's say after a round or more of feeling disappointed and overwhelmed, you became aware that it might have something to do with the letter you got from your bank manager. Something new showing up is called an *aspect*. When a new aspect arises, create a new set-up statement, followed by tapping rounds. Identify what feelings it brings up. Score it and start afresh, repeating the new set-up statement three times while tapping the karate chop point.

| | |
|---|---|
| Karate chop: | 'Even though I was so upset with the letter from the bank manager and decided to eat a biscuit, I accept myself just the way I am' x 3 times |
| Eyebrow: | 'This feeling of anger at the bank manager' |
| Side of Eye: | 'This feeling of struggling with my payments and never having enough money and then eating a whole packet of biscuits' |
| Under Eye: | 'I hate the feeling of having no money' |
| Under Nose: | 'This feeling of disappointment in myself' |
| Under Mouth: | 'This 10 out of 10 feeling of disappointment with myself and having no money' |
| Collarbone: | 'It's not fair' |
| Under Arm: | 'Having no money is no joke' |
| Top of Head: | 'I'm so sick of feeling disappointed with myself and my financial affairs' |
| Score | Deep breath, hands on heart, score out of 10 |

Follow with a few rounds of tapping, updating what you say as new feelings or awarenesses come to mind. It is the incremental understanding, the peeling back of layers that reveals the underlying cause. At the end of each round take a deep breath and write down the score. You may be surprised at the journey on which a few rounds of tapping will take you.

Just a quick word about intense feelings: if at any point you feel overwhelmed with emotion, simply stop tapping, place your hands on your heart and take a few deep breaths until you are calm enough to resume.

## To summarise before you roll up the sleeves and get tapping

1. Sit upright with feet flat on the floor.
2. Choose your most pressing issue.
3. Rate the intensity on a scale of 1 – 10.
4. Craft a 'setup statement' and reminder phrase. The setup is the 'even though' part, the reminder phrase is the issue.
5. Take three deep, slow breaths into your heart-space.
6. Tap on karate chop point while repeating out loud the setup statement three times.
7. Tap through the system of points while saying your reminder phrase. Tap five or six times per point.
8. Once you've finished tapping a round, take a deep breath.
9. Rate the intensity of your issue 1 – 10 again to check progress, and write it down.
10. Repeat and adapt as necessary to expose the issue and get the relief you desire.

What is bothering you the most right now?

What is the most pressing issue in your life? } Write down and score it out of 10

It helps to be as *specific* as you can

'I have a pain in my shoulder' becomes

'I have a sharp pain in my left shoulder when I lift my arm'

The setup statement could be:

'Even though I have this sharp pain in my left shoulder when I lift my arm, I accept myself right now.'

Let's create a scenario and do some rounds of tapping.

Identify WHO, WHY, WHAT and WHEN and your FEELINGS.

Let's make John the subject. Asking WHY am I mad at John helps create the mental picture of who was involved, when it happened, what I felt in my body. Connecting with the experience allows me to rewire my brain's original response using the whole organ. Focus on the feeling or visualise a picture of what happened (or is happening) and describe it.

The setup statement for John might be: 'Even though I'm mad at John because of what he says and does when he's been drinking, I love and accept myself' or 'I'm OK' or another phrase of self-acceptance.

My preference when working with a client is to have them tap and repeat what I say as we each tap on ourselves. Some practitioners tap on the client, who repeats the phrase the practitioner says. It's the tapping that works in combination with the statements, not who is doing the tapping. For a thorough treatise on tapping, I would recommend Nick Ortner's *The Tapping Solution* or Jessica Ortner's *The Tapping Solution for Weight Loss & Body Confidence*.

Once you've got the hang of tapping and speaking, you can vary your reminder phrase to mirror the variety of things you feel about a situation. Just describe honestly what it is you're feeling. You can't get it wrong; repeating the phrase or introducing new thoughts merely reflects the breadth of frustration you're feeling. For example:

| | |
|---|---|
| Score: | Intensity score: 7 or 8 out of 10 |
| Karate chop: | Even though John annoys me when he's been drinking, I deeply and completely accept myself |
| | Even though I've been feeling so much frustration and anger towards John and his drinking, I deeply and completely accept myself |
| | Even though John's drinking drives me crazy, I choose to release these feelings now, and I accept myself right here, right now |
| Eyebrow: | These feelings of annoyance and anger… |
| Side of Eye: | They're driving me crazy… |
| Under Eye: | Part of me can't stand him… |
| Under Nose: | …and what he does when he drinks… |
| Under Mouth: | It's so annoying… |
| Collarbone: | And makes me feel completely mad… |
| Under Arm: | I don't want to feel these feelings… |
| Top of Head: | But I do and they drive me crazy |

*Back to the eyebrow…*

| | |
|---|---|
| Eyebrow: | If I let go of this frustration and anger… |
| Side of Eye: | Then I'm tolerating his behaviour… |
| Under Eye: | And I don't want to do that |
| Under Nose: | I want it to stop |
| Under Mouth: | I want him to stop annoying me... |
| Collarbone: | His irresponsible behaviour.. |
| Under Arm: | These annoying feelings that are so persistent... |
| Top of head: | I wonder if I can let them go?... |
| Score: | 4 |

When the score gets to 1 or 2, try seeing the situation differently, perhaps:

*Introduce the possibility for change:*

| | |
|---|---|
| Eyebrow: | I wonder if I can ignore him... |
| Side of Eye: | And release the frustration and anger... |
| Under Eye: | It's time to let these feelings go... |
| Under Nose: | It really doesn't matter to me what he does... |
| Under Mouth: | And I'm losing out by feeling angry and annoyed... |
| Collarbone: | Releasing these feelings from my body... |
| Under Arm: | Letting them go now... |
| Top of Head: | Letting them go now... |

Tune in to the feeling of annoyance again, on the 1-10 scale, where is it now?

The following somewhat abbreviated case study illustrates how a number of insights can rise to the surface through tapping. In this particular case I combined tapping with drawing, where imagery or symbolism side-stepped the left, logical side of the brain by being processed through the creative, right hemisphere.

The client was a 42 year old mother of two with a career and a husband. She felt frustrated and helpless because of her lack of assertiveness. She saw herself as always helping others, pleasing everyone but herself, both at home and at work. She felt burnt out, was frustrated and lacked motivation.

Since being promoted to associate director at her place of work, she had not experienced the authority or respect she felt was her due. Instead she felt she was not being heard, meetings were being conducted in her absence when she should have been present. She felt she was only nominally a director; she felt overlooked and taken for granted.

With blank sheets of paper and a rainbow of felt pens in front of her, I asked what her most pressing issue was. She spoke about her lack of assertiveness and the symbolism she used was 'paddling her own canoe'. Her score on frustration and resentment was 10.

Using her own words, I asked her to represent it on paper. She outlined a boat with jagged-line water representing rapids. We tapped on what it felt like to be paddling this rough water alone and 'constantly trying to get out of the rapids'. Tap – down from 10 to 8.

As the session progressed, so did her representations: her water became smoother and she added a second boat on which there were matchstick people on perfectly flat water – her work colleagues. She felt the river was taking her along rather than being in control. While they were enjoying the scenery, she was paddling hard and not getting anywhere. A score of 8.

She was feeling more able to pull closer to the other boat but needed to know when to 'stick her oar in' to stop the boat rather than letting it take her into the fast-moving tide. 6 or 7.

She drew the river narrowing. She would have to control the boat, steer it better, use her paddle to direct its course. 5 out of 10.

She felt she would welcome another person in the boat with her, someone with whom she could enjoy things, like the scenery and landscape. Perhaps even have a picnic. 3 out of 10.

Her overall realisation at this point in the session was that she needed balance. Life was hurtling by. She needed more family time on that beach, not just two weeks a year. She wanted to spend time enjoying her family rather than ensuring they were dropped at music or basketball on time. 2 out of 10.

We ventured to the other boat with its four matchstick people – the company directors. She was in her canoe doing all the work – pushing hard, bringing in the business, while they were standing around. Back up to scoring 10 out of 10.

She realised that she needed to stop thinking she was in any way less important. She needed to demonstrate, and they needed to see her on the boat with them. Tap, tap, tap. 6 out of 10.

'They pull me onto their boat when they need me – it's them and us'. She wanted to be on the boat with them, 'not slaving away in second class'. 5 out of 10. Tap, tap, tap 2 out of 10.

Numerous insights were being generated: she needed to act more as a leader, less as a doer, and felt resentful and bitter. She saw herself as a puppet with strings. She cut the strings. Back up to 7 or 8 out of 10 down and down to 2 after several more rounds of fresh awareness and tapping.

The process had enabled her to identify her need for autonomy, visibility, to be heard, to be more assertive and to be more in control, without the need to sacrifice herself for everyone else's benefit. She saw that she had the freedom to decide on and prioritise her needs, to stay and own her space, or to walk out the door and design her own career. 1 out of 10.

As can be seen by a peek into how a tapping session can unfold, the intensity of what is being tapped on is not always linear. What often happens is that a feeling of anger may uncover disappointment, injustice may become sadness or guilt, with scores reflecting the up and down the shifting nature of things. Or one memory can open up others which raise different emotions. The true skill of the practitioner is to identify and capture each new image/feeling/shift/pain being experienced and tap through it until it reaches a 0, 1 or 2.

Clearing one blockage, perhaps a lack of confidence, can have a ripple effect on that same emotion in different circumstances, the root of which had been lodged deep in the subconscious mind at an early age. Unblocking the energy that creates a lack of confidence may restore the energy flow, which allows the person to experience their 'eureka!' moment.

Tapping can help us to understand this process and see those events for what they are – things that happened in the past. People have tapped their way out of PTSD and other debilitating conditions. We now have an opportunity to DIY our own healing of body, mind and spirit. As in Traditional Chinese Medicine, where the patient has an active role in their own healing process, so we can become DIY practitioners to alter the trajectories of our health and wellbeing.

# 18 Matrix Reimprinting

As with any evolving practice, EFT led to the rather cumbersome-sounding intervention called Matrix Reimprinting. While EFT and Matrix Reimprinting both use tapping, Matrix Reimprinting takes the procedure a step further. This chapter will explain what Matrix Reimprinting is and provides case studies to show how it works in practice.

The theoretical physicist, Max Planck, won the Nobel Prize in Physics in 1918 based on his theory that we are all connected by a unified field of energy known as the Universe or Matrix.[154]

The energy healing practice of Matrix Reimprinting really excites me. It would seem to be the container that holds time, providing for a continuity between the experiences of our present, the past and the future.[155] It grew out of EFT and was developed by Englishman Karl Dawson and continues to evolve. The key difference between EFT and Matrix Reimprinting is that while EFT/tapping unblocks the emotional charge and allows energy to flow, Matrix Reimprinting actually changes the memory. Dawson joined up the dots between the power of beliefs, the placebo effect, scientific evidence and how the mind-body stores trauma. It is beliefs that touch every aspect of our lives, from *in utero* and onwards. Any belief that shows up to limit or downgrade our potential can be revisited and rewritten with Matrix Reimprinting.

The principle underlying Matrix Reimprinting is that the frozen fragments that break away during Small t or Big T trauma remain connected to us in the form of Energetic Consciousness Holograms (ECHOS).

Carl Jung's *Shadow* and Robert Scaer's *trauma capsules* describe something similar to an ECHO's frozen fragments. Jung considered personality to be composed of a number of interacting systems: the ego, the personal unconscious and the collective unconscious. Described variously as the Shadow, ECHO or Trauma Capsule, these fragments form a concept, a construct or archetype that exists both externally and internally, universally and individually within our culture and within the human psyche. Aspects of the self that we avoid usually contain within them tremendous energy and wisdom.[156]

Referred to as the ECHO in Matrix Reimprinting, the bottom line is that the shock of past trauma remains in our energy field until we discharge it using specific protocols. Once discharged, the Reimprinting part of Matrix Reimprinting is the process by which a new vision, wisdom or belief is installed to replace the discharged image to render it obsolete – similar to reframing.

In EFT the subject of the tapping is the client. In Matrix Reimprinting, the subject of tapping is the ECHO – the client at a younger age.

Perhaps a short case study will help with understanding the process.

## Joe's Fear of Winning

*Matrix Reimprinting Practitioner Susie Shelmerdine*

Joe is a professional golfer who approached me about using Matrix Reimprinting to improve his score. He had previously seen sports psychologists and cognitive therapists to aid his 'mental game', with some success. He remained openly sceptical about the Matrix Reimprinting process to improve his performance.

During his initial consultation I noticed that he mentioned that he was in awe of his coach and felt pride in playing against others whom he admired. His language did not show he believed he could equal if not surpass these other players. I asked him how it would feel to win against them and he replied hesitantly that it would be fantastic. Through further investigation, it was established that he had always thought he was an average player – good, but nothing special.

Joe told me how one of his idols had given him praise about his game. He did not think it was genuine and thought that he was just being nice. He had a specific picture of this memory, so I asked him to freeze the picture and tap on himself in it.

In the picture, Joe looked quiet, withdrawn and completely lacking in confidence. He introduced himself to his younger self (his ECHO) and explained who he was and why he was there. As he tapped on his younger self, he learned that there was a fear of not meeting his potential. He learned that there was a benefit to not winning – if he won he would have to make a speech.

From there we were led to three related memories: the time Joe froze during a winning speech, the time he stumbled on his words in an award ceremony, and a school presentation which hadn't gone well. Joe replaced each memory with a happy and positive picture. I also gave him homework to do for the next session.

Joe had two competitions in the two weeks following our session. He came third in the first one, and was pleased with this result, but he now wanted to win. He decided to write his winning speech and practise it, tapping on the fear. We used the Matrix

Future-Self Reimprinting protocol, and he imagined crowds applauding and his idols congratulating him.

The second competition he won. It was the best he had ever played. His speech went well afterwards and he also went on to win a further game.

At the time of writing this case study, he is only a third of the way through his competitions for the year and has already surpassed his personal target.

Reproduced with permission: www.susieshelmerdine.com

In Matrix Reimprinting there is no attempt to deny that the trauma happened. The aim is to discover the belief formed in that UDIN (Unexpected, Dramatic, Isolating, No strategy) moment (see pg 77) and dissolve the ECHO's energy fragment. By resourcing the ECHO in the matrix with their own and the practitioner's backing, the ECHO is empowered to make different decisions. For example, if the ECHO is feeling frightened, take them to a safe place, or switch on the light if they are afraid of the dark. Support and resource the ECHO to overcome their challenge. The ECHO can resolve unfinished business in whatever way feels right by rescripting the event or otherwise altering it in a way that removes the emotional charge.

Joe's previous desire to improve his 'mental game' as a golf professional had not delivered results. With Matrix Reimprinting he was able to track back to three occasions when his ECHO had been stressed and humiliated by addressing an audience – an event totally unrelated to golf which golf coaches would have overlooked. His subconscious was ensuring that he would not have to deliver a Winner's Speech and thus be humiliated yet again. With this new awareness, preparing for future success became easy, already evidenced by Joe exceeding his personal target.

A point worth noting here is that, just as a jenga tower collapses when enough pieces have been removed to destabilise it, so, too, can the belief formed at the time of the trauma be collapsed when enough small t or big T-related incidents have been identified and removed. Matrix Reimprinting discharges the misplaced belief and installs something more empowering that is created by that which feels right or most appropriate by the resourced ECHO, the client's younger self.

The process of Matrix Reimprinting is a simple and non-invasive method of getting to the core belief caused by the trauma that lies behind the story which was unconsciously created to protect the person from further pain. It addresses the root cause, not the symptom. However, it is a procedure that needs to be managed by a trained and qualified practitioner.

As with EFT, Matrix Reimprinting protocols are in place to safeguard the individual from reliving the experience which caused the trauma. Where serious issues are being addressed, there are strict protocols for dissociation (distancing or disconnecting from being re-traumatised) as protection from the original memory. A simple example might be a belief formed that 'the world is a dangerous place', 'I'm worthless', 'I was to blame' or 'I'm powerless'. Continued use of this filter in multiple different situations would render the person vulnerable and less than resilient. Remembering that not all soldiers get PTSD, it is worth noting that it is not the event that causes the trauma, but the belief or decision the person/ECHO made about themselves or their life at the time that is key.

## Intergenerational inheritance

A baby *in utero* receives its nutrients and everything else from its mother in a constant stream of molecules and hormones that reflect what is happening in the mother's world. In other words, whatever signals the mother is receiving and transmitting are fed to the baby through the placenta. It follows that a pregnant woman whose environment has chronic levels of stress, such as in a warzone, or who might have toxic habits like smoking or drug use, will create an *in utero* environment very different from someone who meditates regularly and is nutritionally balanced. The fertilized egg is affected by its *in utero* exposure.

Genetics and our DNA do not begin and end with us, but are blueprints passed on to subsequent generations.[157]In her book *Heal Your Birth Heal Your Life*, Sharon King describes how all the ova required throughout a female's lifetime are present while she is *in utero*. What happens to her in the womb and at birth has far-reaching consequences for her own life and those of her children yet unborn. King has developed a process called Matrix Birth Reimprinting, which allows males and females to deal with unplanned pregnancy, *in utero* experiences, traumatic birth, or issues they might be carrying which belong to their mothers.

The following case study of a client traces their ECHO stream to their own birth, and illustrates how their story ultimately makes sense to them.

**Seamus had pervasive feelings of not being good enough and not being heard**

Seamus (35) approached me because his life seemed without direction or purpose. His partner of sixteen years had died two years previously, but he had been unable to grieve publicly because, apart from a few close friends, the relationship had remained in the closet. Soon afterward he had left his job due to stress. He had worked in several positions since, but at that stage was in receipt of social welfare benefit. Over a period we had had a number of tapping sessions and had successfully worked through his grief and other issues related to his sexuality, to the point when he came out to his family. However, one overriding belief, in spite of more than pulling his weight in the family and at work, was that he never felt good enough. Seamus was curious to learn what a Matrix Birth Reimprinting session would reveal.

The youngest of four children, at five months of age the family had relocated to a house in the town in which Seamus subsequently grew up. The family was largely self-sufficient in growing, harvesting and preserving their own produce from a neighbouring allotment. As a child and into his teens, the majority of Seamus's time not spent at school was spent working on the allotment, doing household chores or homework. He struggled with reading and writing, but made it through school, and went on to college to qualify as a chef.

Seamus grew up feeling resentful, mostly around not having a right to speak or be heard, and the belief that he was 'not entitled to' a range of things. He was conscious never to make a fuss, always felt compelled to do what was right and 'just get on with it'. His abiding drive was to prove himself, to justify his existence.

Seamus had been born at home after a difficult labour: in a breach presentation, his mother was left to struggle alone while the doctor took advantage of his father's bottle of whiskey in the kitchen. The labour was prolonged and difficult. The bonding process did not happen, as he was whisked away to be 'cleaned up' to allow his mother time to recover. The belief his ECHO had formed, he realised, was that he had to manage on his own.

We started with some general tapping on not being good enough, and not being heard, adding aspects such as his inability to move in the womb, as well as his need to feel safe and loved. Travelling back down his timeline, Seamus stopped at his five month old babyself (his ECHO). Something didn't feel right, but he wasn't able to identify what it was. We travelled back earlier in time, to the point of his birth, but he wanted to go back still earlier. He realised how distressed and stuck his ECHO felt in the womb, and how fearful he was of the process of being born. Seamus communicated with his babyself, asking what he needed. Rather than go to the hospital, his babyself chose to stay in the family home but that his father should be present at the birth to welcome him.

In rescripting his birth in the Matrix, he dismissed the doctor and instead his mother was attended by her mother and a sister who was a nurse. In a breach presentation he felt stuck in the birth canal; his ECHO chose to go back into the womb and make whatever body adjustment was necessary for a normal delivery. This was accomplished with ease, his father catching him and placing him on his mother's chest.

Seamus could feel and hear the sound of his mother's heartbeat and felt the love of being wanted. He breathed in the smell of flowers and could hear the dawn chorus as he bonded with his mother, his father's arms around them both. This was the picture we reimprinted: feeling welcomed, loved and secure.

From there we travelled forward in time to the five month old ECHO. His babyself felt agitated, sick in the throat, neglected and scared. He could see his babyself in a Moses basket in a room with all the noise and activity of a house-move going on about him. The words that came to him were strange – 'You're a bother'. He was surprised as it wasn't a phrase he would have normally used. Joining the dots between being a bother and the historical event of the family move happened exactly five months to the day of his birth. Believing himself a bother, 'in the way' and being 'an irritant' suddenly made sense. He was astonished at the impact his five-month-old perception had had on his life.

Seamus checked in with his babyself about what he would like. He needed to be held, loved and reassured. Seamus's mother cradled and rocked him on a bright, rainbow-coloured beanbag in a room flooded with sunlight. He experienced contentment and joy, his eyes closed. His babyself felt his mother's love and her delight. It was all they both needed before both drifting off to sleep. This was the picture we reimprinted.

In a follow-up call with Seamus some six months later we discussed his tangled beliefs of not wanting to be a 'disturbance', of having to manage alone and not being heard – beliefs that still showed up in his life – but with one significant difference: he was now conscious of what was going on and could exercise choice.

Putting others' needs ahead of his own, he recognised, was a symptom of not wanting to disturb them. Being alone had forged his spirit of independence and he no longer needed the approval of others. The insights had freed him up to change his mind, and adapt his thinking and attitude to his expanding life. He had made the decision to study for a degree – a big step for somebody who had believed they did not have the ability to attend university. He recognised the need for further work to completely resolve his limiting beliefs, but the insight had freed him up to enjoy a richer and fuller life.

Beliefs that have had years of practice, have been hardwired into superhighways, are not wiped out in one session. As with any muscle training, strengthening works with resistance and persistence.

# Section 4 Spirituality

A quote from author Elizabeth Lesser is 'Spirituality is a brave search for the truth about existence, fearlessly peering into the mysterious nature of life'.

Spirituality is working your way through the dark until you see the chink of light. It is striving to find purpose in life. It is about overcoming the drag of disappointment and building muscles of courage, trust, optimism, laughter, friendship, joy and persistence.

Spirituality is concerned with the heart and soul. It does not necessarily separate itself from religion: religion can be spiritual and spirituality can be religious. Spirituality, as used here, is expressing our individual qualities even as we are part of the cosmic whole. It is our way of loving, accepting and relating to ourselves, people and the world around us with authenticity and openness. Spirituality retreats when voices of anger or pride or jealousy are loudest, but can emerge with greater confidence and purpose when we give ourselves the gifts of quiet, compassion and reflective time.

# Body and Soul

In terms of the beliefs, feelings, dogmas and practices that define relations between ourselves and the sacred or divine, who knows when or where the separation of body and soul came about. Ascetics across the centuries and religions have practiced acts of denial in a bid to achieve purity of thought and transcendence, with celibacy, isolation and fasting being common. These practices suggest that denial of bodily desires would or could lead to attaining states of ecstasy or enlightenment. Hardly any religion has been without at least some traces or features of asceticism, based on the premise that body and soul are somehow separate. Using this concept, soul could develop only at the expense of the body. Self-flagellation and self-laceration were punishments to cleanse the body of its passions. In this divide of the spirit from the body, the body was deemed the gatekeeper of the soul.

By contrast, indigenous African, Asian, Aboriginal and Native American peoples, while diverse in language, culture and place, nevertheless held common beliefs about body and soul; there was no separation. Their understanding was of a world where spiritual and material matters worked in harmony. The child knew who they were in relation to family, tribe and ancestors, the land, plants and animals, weather, seasons and spirits. Each was recognised and respected as individual, while still being a part of the whole. It did not mean that there were no imbalances or that war and territory were not fought over. It meant there was an acceptance of the individual's place and their part in the wider scheme of life and survival.

You will be in no doubt that the ideas presented throughout this book are those of coherence between internal and external occurrences; between body and mind, emotions, beliefs, relationships and the external environment. It is about integrating the internal with the external; collaboration not separation.

Wellbeing is wholebeing, encompassing physical, emotional and mental dimensions, as well as social, community, intellectual and spiritual. Spiritual wellbeing, if we consider our place in the universal scheme, is how we honour ourselves as necessary and integral parts of a wider and greater whole. This doesn't require us to be perfect in every area to be spiritually well; imperfections or disease do not lessen our capacity to be spiritual. The key is for each of us to explore what we believe to be our meaning and purpose, and use this as the compass by which we navigate and direct our lives. Being spiritual, then, is not a destination, but a perennial, day-by-day process of adjusting and correcting actions, decisions, thoughts and beliefs according to our own guiding star, our own higher purpose.

## Community

As humans we need a sense of belonging, that which connects us to the many relationships we develop. We are members of many communities – family, work, neighbourhood, club, choir, team supporters – an endless collection of groups we move in and out of and within. Community is essential to our wellbeing, where resources are shared by us as both givers and receivers. Contribution to something greater than ourselves is a form of transcendence, an expression of giving as well as receiving in balance.

Communities also carry risks. We can become too comfortable or complacent, regarding the world beyond this or that community with prejudice or suspicion. The 'community' referred to for spiritual growth is one of tolerance, nurturing human connection to overcome such multiple and limited barriers.

Altruism, compassion and authenticity come into it. There are situations too numerous to count where individuals have performed heroic acts with no thought for their personal safety, either as a single act or in continuous regular sacrifice. However, it is the daily challenge, the moment-by-moment decision-making while navigating our lives that calls on our core resources. It is this resilience of spirit, of who we are every moment of every day in spite of challenges or weariness, that determines our individual heroism and membership of our various communities.

## Growing in spirituality

Bombarded with injustice, fear and disarray in the news and in our lives, it is easy to understand why so much is out of balance. A call for stability, starting on the inside, is how we can develop positive spiritual practice. Again, it isn't about big events or waiting for the right moment, but rather it is about noticing everyday opportunities as they present themselves. Simple yet effective ways to incorporate spirituality into our daily lives are numerous: we just need to slow down and find the good, the humour, the perfection, the irony or simplicity in small things.

From his book *Awaken the Giant Within,* Anthony Robbins suggests three questions to ask ourselves each evening.

– What have I given today?
– What did I learn today?
– How has today added to the quality of my life or how can I use today as an investment in my future?

You may remember from earlier that an exercise such as this actually changes the brain. May I suggest one further step to this practice: have this list beside your bathroom mirror and read it as you brush your teeth each morning, but phrased in the future tense. What can I give today? What can I learn today? and What can I do today that will add to the quality of my life? Priming your mind to anticipate how you will behave will alert your awareness in the most spiritual way possible. Dwelling on the answers before going to sleep, being accountable to yourself each day is the spin-off and a double whammy for your spiritual growth.

We can choose to do exercises like this or not. Even sound suggestions will not force us to do anything we don't want to do. But the naked fact is this: everything we avoid or every challenge we face are the universe's gift to us to learn something about ourselves and provides the potential for growth. What we do with these opportunities is our choice. As the Buddhist saying goes, the teacher will appear when the student is ready. Many such occasions occur in this book. Either the teacher or our own up-to-now silent wisdom can provide a flash of something that can change our direction. It simply depends on whether or if the student, meaning you, is ready.

## Finding the Centre

The notion of growing in spirituality harks back to our Circle of Influence on page 122, where efforts to manage our thinking can support or undermine our integrity. We can choose to spend our energies on measures that will significantly contribute to self-efficacy and ultimately our spirituality, to discover and live by our core values or fall back as victims to the wills and whims of others. Indeed, even adopting one lesson from these pages, whether learning a few assertive communication techniques, being clearer on personal boundaries, or applying the E+R=O formula, will contribute to wellbeing and spiritual growth.

In Newtonian mechanics, centrifugal force arises when a force acts upon mass or matter to cause it to deviate from its straight-line path. If you have ever been on a merry-go-round, then you have experienced centrifugal force. The centre is the still point, while just beyond that is where the energetic force is at play.

The mind can be likened to a merry-go-round, or what Siegel describes as the Wheel of Awareness.[158] The hub of the wheel is the centre, the still point from which radiate the spokes, connecting it to the outer rim. The rim represents everything we pay attention to: thoughts and feelings, dreams and desires, memories, awareness of the outside world and sensations from the body. Being on the rim (as with the merry-go-round) requires us to hang on for dear life or face certain hurt, knowing that the faster the spin, the greater the injury.

Our attention focused on the rim determines our state of mind. Whether distracted or busy or angry, our attention is locked onto whatever is most pressing on the rim. Distraction leads to numerous states of imbalance, and we are trapped in habits of the past which come at a price.

The hub or centre is the part of our brain (the prefrontal cortex or team captain) that allows left and right, upstairs and downstairs brains to connect with our heart and work optimally. It is where our awareness resides, the part of ourselves that allows us to connect with the outside world with awareness and understanding.

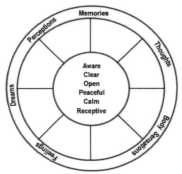

**Adapted with permission from page 94 of the book** *The Whole-Brain Child:*
*12 Revolutionary Strategies to Nurture Your Child's Developing Mind*
**by Daniel J. Siegel and Tina Payne Bryson (Random House, 2011)**

Once we recognise that we are not our rim, the rim of perceptions, thoughts, feelings, dreams or body sensations, but are rather responding to what is happening outside of us, we can better learn to control where we place our attention. Good aspects also reside on the rim, but our attention spends more time on the demands. Time spent in the hub is when we take control and manage the manageables. In our hurry to meet deadlines, fulfil obligations, manage ten balls in the air, keep our eye on what's happening next door so that we can keep up, we are so busy 'hanging on' that we have little time to pause and reflect on what is driving us. The rim is not the hub, *it is not who we are.* Visualising the wheel in this way will help individuals realise their ability to separate their hub from the rim – themselves from their distractions.

Sometimes easier said than done, we may wonder how on earth to get back to the hub under the burden of responsibilities, everyday tasks, finances, children, job or the row you just had with your friend. As with everything, we improve only with practice. With practice we begin to notice our tendency to focus on the rim elements that shout the loudest.

In that split second of awareness, take a deep breath, then a second and third – imagine, if you can, even breathing into your heart while placing your hands over it. In those moments you have connected with your core. The problem will not have gone away, but you have taken control and returned to your hub. And the more you practice, the more quickly you will be able to connect with your core as well as extend the duration of still-point time. The more your practice, the more frequent the body-mind connection. Otherwise known as training. It will begin to plug the leaks and fill your core.

Understanding, wisdom and insight – all ingredients of spirituality – are not destinations. They are moment-by-moment events that are unceasing, from one challenge or thought to the next. Once we realise our attention is on the experience or drama, emotion or thought, we are better equipped to manage it. It means facing obstacles and taking whatever detours or actions are needed with a mind that accepts whatever is presented in self-honouring and authentic ways.

Learning techniques to return to our hub, to feel the emotions emanating from more productive rim points such as accepting that we are... smart, compassionate, get on well with our friends because we understand their needs – the unique aspects that make us who we are – we take charge. We can learn not to be right or have the last word – habits on our rim that make us believe we are stuck with the person we believe ourselves to be. Let's begin to choose more compassionate rim points to alleviate the feelings of inadequacy. Let's internalise the positives to create a resilient hub that will ultimately change the structure of the heart, the brain and soul.

## Getting back to your hub

This is an exercise or meditation to expand your spirituality through spending more time in your still place, your hub, adapted from the Spirit Voyage website and copied with permission from Arielle Schwartz, PhD[159].Sit comfortably with your back straight, both feet on the floor, legs uncrossed. First with your eyes open, try letting your attention go to the far wall. Just notice your attention as you let it go to the dresser/table/picture. Then gently look to the left and focus on what you see. Now follow your attention as it goes to the window. Let it come back to the dresser/table/picture. Can you bring it up close as if it were at arm's length? Notice how you are able to direct your attention to different places.

Become aware of the sounds around you – traffic, people talking, dog barking – just become aware of the sounds and let them fill your awareness. Don't dwell on them or think up a story about them. Just notice what it is you are hearing.

Now bring your attention inside yourself. Get a sense inside your-self, of your body. Take a slow and easy breath in through your nose to the count of three or four, whatever is comfortable, feeling your chest expand. Hold the breath to a count of three or four and then release it to a count of three or four. Feel the air moving softly through your nostrils as it returns to the atmosphere.

Become aware of your breath as it travels in and out in waves. Where do you feel your breath the most – in your nostrils? On your top lip? The rise and fall of your chest or abdomen? Wherever you feel it, let your awareness ride the wave of that feeling as you breathe in and out. If your attention wanders, gently bring it back to riding the wave of your breath.

Become aware of your feet in contact with the floor, your lower legs. Knees. Thighs. Pelvis and lower abdomen. Chest. Left arm, left hand. Right arm, right hand. Jaw. Throat. Tongue. Eyes.

Become aware of any sensation you may feel anywhere in your body - maybe in your arms, chest, fists – of pain or tension. Just iden-tify where it is, name it but don't dwell on it. Watch it as if on the rim, then gently return your attention to your hub, following your breath in and out.

When you come to notice, as often happens, that your mind has wandered and become lost in a thought or a memory, a feeling, a wor-ry, when you notice that, just take note of it and gently, lovingly, return your awareness to your breath, to your hub – and follow it as you breath in and out.

What else might be going on that you can you see on the rim of your wheel? Name it, observe it without emotional involvement, then let it go and return to your breath.

Let your attention return to your breathing and follow the breath to reground yourself in the calm and peaceful place in the deepest part of you. From this place it's possible to become aware of the activities of your mind or sensations in your body without being swept away by them.

What feelings or thoughts can you name on the rim of your wheel? Name them in your mind if you can *without feeling them*. Gently accept the thought or feeling as you name it, and return to conscious breathing in and out.

Notice that everything going on in your mind is NOT who you are; you are more than your thoughts, more than your feelings. You can have those thoughts and feelings and with your 'observer self' also be able to just notice them with the wisdom that they are not your identity. They are simply one part of your mind's experience, like 'thinking' or 'feeling', 'remembering' or 'worrying'. Just take note of them as they come and go, then gently let them float out of awareness.

This exercise can be used in anticipation of an event, like an exam or any other issue that might cause anxiety. It can be used as a daily practice: controlling anxiety teaches self-management. It can also be used after an event, where anger or fear or humiliation are named and seen as only one aspect of our wider identity; recognising the temporary nature of changing emotions.

Regular practice brings about a balance between our left and right, upstairs and downstairs brains, and when we integrate this with our heart, it strengthens our core, our connection with others and prepares us for greater spiritual wellbeing.

This final chapter suggests that spirituality is a state of mind that responds to external demands or internal reactions via our thoughts, beliefs and practices. The more we return to the still point, our hub, the more we recognise and value our worth to ourselves and others.

In spite of the many technological ways of communication, we need authentic heart connection with ourselves and our tribe; to be understood, accepted, seen, heard and loved. We can raise the bar on all aspects of wellbeing with conscious attention. It is a worthy cause. We are worthy causes. You are a worthy cause.

The notion that we can change who we want to be is a concept we may hardly have thought about. Or perhaps feel that it is available to others, but certainly not to ourselves. If there's one message apparent from what I have learned over the years, it is that change is hard but is achievable by any- and everyone once they put their minds to what they want to let go of and what they desire to replace it with.

Brain plasticity teaches us that we are not stuck with the grades/job/partner/ability to communicate that we have accepted as our lot. The Human Genome Project and epigenetics point out that it is the environment, and not our DNA, that sets the limits on what we can change or achieve. Yes, there are hereditary conditions that may limit us, but the majority of what holds us back are the beliefs and habits borne of a lifetime of practice.

The idea of being an active and proactive participant in our own health and wellbeing is not new, but making a decision to engage with ourselves in envisioning a new future might be.

This book is a call to take charge and take responsibility. No one else will, except, perhaps, that someone else has their own agenda for you. Decide what you want. Work with your Higher Self – your heart, your and integrated brain. Engage with your doctor as an equal member of your health team. Engage with a wider cohort of people who can and will help. Read. Join support groups. Become a giver and a taker of wisdom and learning. Try one new thing you have learned from this book and see how far you can take the adventure. My wish for you is to have fun on your journey, and to take pride in each small step you take toward wellbeing from the inside out.

# About the Author

A Guide to Wellbeing *from the inside out* is Hazel Boylan's first book, having published short stories in two collections. She draws on the techniques and skillsets acquired through her many years working as a personal development trainer, career and life coach and energy health practitioner. Trained in EFT, Matrix Reimprinting and Life Coaching, Hazel helps individuals free themselves of negative habits and self-limiting beliefs by identifying and releasing energy blocks to allow their transition to greatly empowered futures. Her knowledge, intuition and creativity inspire others to be resourceful, to find their mojo, and to take responsibility for their growth.

Hazel holds an Honours Degree in Psychology from Trinity College Dublin and an MSc in Work and Organisational Psychology from Dublin City University.

To find out more about Hazel and the services she offers, visit http://www.hazelboylan.com or on Facebook at: EFT and Matrix Reimprinting with Hazel Boylan.

# Please Review this Book

Thank you for taking the time to read this book. If you found it helpful, please help me spread the message to others who may be seeking this information. Please visit Amazon, or the platform where you purchased this book to write a review. A review can also be left on Goodreads. This matters because most potential readers first judge a book by what others have to say. An honest review would be most appreciated.

I can also be contacted via my website http://www.hazelboylan.com/

Connect with me also on Facebook: EFT and Matrix Reimprinting with Hazel Boylan.

# Recommended TED Talks and YouTube Videos

## Brain

**Jill Bolte Taylor, My Stroke of Insight** – 20:12 minutes
TED Talks
Neuroanatomist Jill Bolte Taylor had an opportunity few brain scientists would wish for: one morning, she realized she was having a massive stroke. As it happened – as she felt her brain functions slip away one by one, speech, movement, understanding – she studied and remembered every moment. This is a powerful story about how our brains define us and connect us to the world and to one another.

**Lisa Wimberger, How to Rewrite Your Brain's Story** – 8:56 minutes
Ever feel like if your brain was an author, it would be Stephen King? Your brain loves telling stories, especially when they're stressful or traumatic. Lisa Wimberger, Founder of the Neurosculping Institute, explains why your brain does this and explains how you can give your brain a new 'story' to tell

**Dr. Rick Hanson, Hardwiring happiness** – 13:45 minutes
TEDxMarin 2013
Hardwiring Happiness : The Hidden Power of Everyday Experiences on the Modern Brain. How to overcome the Brain's Negativity Bias.

Rick Hanson is a neuropsychologist and the author of Hardwiring Happiness: The New Brain Science of Contentment, Calm, and Confidence, best selling author of Buddha's Brain, founder of the Wellspring Institute for Neuroscience and Contemplative Wisdom and an Affiliate of the Greater Good Science Center at UC Berkeley. He's been an invited speaker at Oxford, Stanford, and Harvard, and taught in meditation centres worldwide.

## Don Vaughn, Neurohacking: rewiring your brain – 20:01 minutes
TEDxUCLA

We've all heard of the phrase "life hack". But have you heard of something called a "brain hack"? Don Vaughn gives us the inside scoop on the amazing powers of the human brain.

## Mel Robbins Discusses the "Five Second Rule" at DMA's &THEN15 – 11:42 minutes

The 5 Second Rule to Change Your Life. In this day and age, there are so many resources available to us as marketers to improve the performance of our campaigns. Here's one that will improve your own performance - as a marketer. In this quick video, CNN contributor and &THEN host, Mel Robbins reprises her critically acclaimed -- and viral, TEDx Talk -- on the Inspiration Stage at &THEN in Boston last October. Watch as she demystifies neuroscience research on the brain and the latest social science research to explain why and how marketers can improve performance every day. You'll learn how to identify the mistakes you're making and learn how to create lasting behavior change within yourself. You'll also discover one radical idea that will forever alter how you approach life.

## Childhood, Early Learning

**Nadine Burke Harris, How childhood trauma affects health across a lifetime** – 16:03 minutes TEDMED

Childhood trauma isn't something you just get over as you grow up. Paediatrician Nadine Burke Harris explains that the repeated stress of abuse, neglect and parents struggling with mental health or substance abuse issues has real, tangible effects on the development of the brain. This unfolds across a lifetime, to the point where those who have experienced high levels of trauma are at triple the risk for heart disease and lung cancer. An impassioned plea for paediatric medicine to confront the prevention and treatment of trauma, head-on.

**Dr Vincent Felitti, How Childhood Trauma Can Make You A Sick Adult** – 7:15 minutes

Big Think and the Mental Health Channel are proud to launch Big Thinkers on Mental Health, a new series dedicated to open discussion of anxiety, depression, and the many other psychological disorders that affect millions worldwide.

**Annie Murphy Paul: What we learn before we're born** – 16:46
TED Talk July 2011

Science writer Annie Murphy Paul talks through new research that shows how much we learn in the womb -- from the lilt of our native language to our soon-to-be-favourite foods.

## Trauma

### Peter Tuerk, Return from Chaos: Treating PTSD – 12:15 minutes
TEDxCharleston

Peter Tuerk, the director of a PTSD program, introduces how we process experiences and trauma. Using examples from his research, he describes how it's possible to process memories and their associated meanings to overcome a traumatic incident. When active avoidance impedes natural recovery the most effective healing is facilitated through treatment designed to limit avoidance and to assist with the processing of relevant information.

### Janet Seahorn, Understanding PTSD's Effects on Brain, Body, and Emotions, TEDxCSU – 15:58 minutes
PTSD disrupts the lives of average individuals as well as combat veterans who have served their country. The person experiencing the trauma often then impacts the lives of his/her family, friends, and workplaces. PTSD does not distinguish between race, age or gender and often goes undiagnosed. Even with proper diagnosis, many individuals do not know where to turn to get help. Society needs to understand the aftermath of trauma especially combat trauma and how to prepare for warriors when they return home.

### Dr Bessel van der Kolk, The Body Keeps the Score: Brain, Mind, and Body in the Healing of Trauma – 1:40:27 minutes
Trauma is a fact of life. Veterans and their families deal with the painful aftermath of combat; one in five Americans has been molested; one in four grew up with alcoholics; one in three couples have engaged in physical violence—the body keeps the score. That's how Dr. Bessel van der Kolk, one of the world's leading experts on develop-

mental trauma, explains how our long-term health and happiness can be compromised by prior exposure to violence, emotional abuse, and other forms of traumatic stress. In his new book, Dr. van der Kolk explores how innovative treatments—ranging from meditation and neurofeedback to yoga, sports, and drama—offer new paths to healing and wellness. A psychiatrist and author of multiple books, his work and perspectives have been featured in The New York Times, on National Public Radio, and in many other media outlets.

## Energy Psychology

**David Gruder - What is Energy Psychology?** – 3:13 minutes

**David Feinstein @ Energy Psychology Conference 2013 PTSD** – 4:53 minutes

David Feinstein states that the conference is "organized around the most important developments in psychology..PTSD " - post traumatic stress disorder, which is an epidemic in the USA especially due the wars Americans got involved with. In his 40 year practice, this is the most important development he as seen. He endorses this conference saying "this conference is probably the best single place you can go for an introduction in this whole area. In fact he sites that "in june of 2013, more than 9 million people did a search for energy psychology methods"

**Tarcher Talks: The Power of Energy Medicine** (4 of 4) 9:21 minutes

David Feinstein, author of The Promise of Energy Psychology, explains how the principles of Energy Medicine can be applied to the field of psychology

**Energy Psychology with Larry King & Dr. George Pratt** 7:30 minutes

Larry King interviews Dr. George Pratt about "Energy Psychology", which is a blend of Western cognitive processes and Eastern healing methods. George Pratt, Ph.D. is a licensed clinical psychologist in private practice for 30+ years, and has served as Chairman of Psychology, Scripps Memorial Hospital, La Jolla for 10 years. He is the co-author of the award-winning bestseller Instant Emotional Healing: Acupressure for the Emotions. He has been a repeat guest on Larry King Live.

## Mind-Body Connection

**Dr. Staci Borkhuis Neuroplasticity - extraordinary health potential** – 16:56 minutes TEDxMinot

In her talk, Dr. Staci Borkhuis discusses living how one can live an extraordinary life by taking control of their own thoughts and actions.

**Janine Shepherd, You are not your body** – 19:01 minutes TEDxKC

Janine Shepherd is a walking paraplegic; she is also a qualified pilot and aerobatics instructor, international speaker and author. Once voted as one of the world's most outstanding and inspirational people, Janine devotes her professional life to empowering others to overcome adversity.

**David Reilly, Human Healing Unlocked: transforming suffering into wellbeing** – 27:24 minutes TEDxFindhornSalon

David Reilly trained as a physician and a GP and evaluated aspects of complementary medicine and mind-body medicine. He approaches medicine and human caring in ways that emphasise the innate healing capacity in people, the factors that modify the healing response, and their interaction in the therapeutic encounter and relationship – ideas adopted as the core of The Fifth Wave document exploring future health in Scotland.

**Danna Pycher, Healing illness with the subconscious mind** – 17:10 minutes TEDxPineCrestSchool

Surviving an accident was the easy part; coping with the chronic pain would prove more difficult. Danna Pycher shares her story about trauma and the transformative insight she gained that allowed her to harness the healing power of the subconscious mind.

**Jeremy Bennett, The Amazing Power of Your Mind** – 10:44 minutes

With nearly 60,000 thoughts per day, you're bound to have plenty of negative ones, right? What you may not realize is the power you hold when it comes to the anxious thoughts and feelings you have on a daily basis. Millions of people suffer from the effects of anxiety as they allow their subconscious minds run their lives. The key to overcoming anxiety is to realize that YOU ARE IN CONTROL. In other words, if you are able to create your anxious responses to situations, you are also able to take them away. The first step to a better life is understanding that your response to scenarios is what causes your anxiety and stress, rather than the situations themselves causing your reactions. Discover the ins and outs of this explosive scientific discovery in this short informative video.

**The Simonton Documentary in progress, youtube** – 6.17 minutes

A radiation oncologist, traditionally trained, talks of the mind-body connection in treating the immune system

## Lifestyle Choices / Diet

### Dr. Terry Wahls, How I Went From Wheelchair To Walking By Changing My Diet – 19:03 minutes

Dr. Terry Wahls was given a diagnosis of MS and told she'd have to spend the rest of her life in a wheelchair. After radically transforming her diet, her outlook, and her medical care, she is now able to walk and ride a bicycle.

### Dr Mark Hyman, Inflammation: How to cool the fire inside you – 6:46 minutes

Is a hidden, smouldering fire in your body coming between you and good health? This week on the UltraWellness blog, Mark Hyman, M.D. explains how inflammation causes chronic disease and weight gain -- and uncovers the link between food allergies and inflammation.

### Dr. Neal Barnard, Power Foods for the Brain - 21:17 minutes

TedX Bismarck

Dr. Barnard has led numerous research studies investigating the effects of diet on diabetes, body weight, and chronic pain, including a groundbreaking study of dietary interventions in type 2 diabetes, funded by the National Institutes of Health. Dr. Barnard has authored over 70 scientific publications as well as 17 books. As president of the Physicians Committee, Dr. Barnard leads programs advocating for preventive medicine, good nutrition, and higher ethical standards in research.

# EFT

### Karl Dawson, EFT Matrix Reimprinting tapping solutions for Anxiety and Abuse – 59:27 minutes

In the session with Karl Dawson, Creator of Matrix Reimprinting, works with a client who exhibits fear and anxiety of standing out in public. The hour long session uncovers past events of emotional, physical and sexual abuse as the underlying reasons behind the anxiety.

### Jenny Johnson, EFT for Sexual Abuse, Using the Movie Technique and Quantum EFT – 52:36 minutes

Client began at 20 out of 10 with a severe trauma of Sexual Abuse and after almost an hour session and uncovering other memories to work on, she was ready for a pleasant lunch at the pub feeling relaxed and peaceful. The trauma was approached gently with the Movie Technique and also using Quantum EFT in time/space/place.

# Matrix Reimprinting

### Sharon King, Matrix Birth Reimprinting Demonstration – 53:18 minutes

Sharon King works with one of her students at the Matrix Birth Reimprinting workshop in Vancouver, BC The traditional EFT Movie Technique is a powerful means to release what has happened to us in the past. Using the Matrix Reimprinting Technique helps to takes this a step further by allowing you to interact with yourself at the time of the event and release the emotions and change the memory to a more positive one.

# Index

**A**

ACES, 101

Acupuncture, 163, 165, 169, 177-180

Acupressure, 177,180,187, 236

Adversity, 100-104, 236

compensating for

Aggression, 37, 38, 99

Alkaline, 31, 152

Alzheimers, 17

Amalgam fillings, 21

Anger, 9,10,12, 20, 35, 39, 48, 52, 68, 71-74, 108, 120, 141, 161, 177, 179, 189, 191-199, 202, 213, 223

Assertiveness, 35-37, 40, 44, 48, 49, 51, 162, 200

Assertive and Unassertive Behaviour, 37-38

Assertive Rights, 42-45

Aura, 169-170

Autoimmune disease, 23, 29

Avoidance, 39, 74, 234


**B**

Barnard, Dr Neal, 238

Beattie, Melanie, Codependent No more, 61, 253, 260

Beck's Cognitive Triad, 110-111

Bernard, Claude, 151, 154, 264

Biofeedback, xiii, 160, 172, 180

Blind spot, 138, 144-145

Body-mind, 15, 76, 107, 165, 169, 220

Bolte Taylor, Jill, 7, 231

Borkhuis, Dr Staci, 236

Boundaries, personal, 51-61

Bowlby, 97

Brain

brain-gut connection, 18, 256, 258

brain-gut axis, 18-19

broken brain, 19-20, 23, 256, 257

corpus callosum, 7

dominant function, 4-5

health, 15-33, 255

integration – horizontal and vertical, 10, 12-13

leaky brain, 19-20

left and right, 5-12, 73, 89, 130, 219, 223

plasticity, 4, 13, 17, 98, 224

upstairs and downstairs, 8-12, 180, 219, 223

whole brain functioning, xii, 10-12, 192,

Buddhist, 7, 157, 218

Bullying, 38, 55, 137, 182, 189


**C**

Callahan, Roger, 179-180

Case study, vii, 181, 199, 204, 206, 208

Cells, 3, 15-18, 26, 31, 98, 100, 154-155, 159-161, 172, 176

Champion, 89, 101-104, 114, 116, 177

Channel 26, 55, 63, 169, 233

Cholesterol, 29, 166

Chronic stress, 101

Circle of Concern, Circle of Influence, 127-129, 141, 155-156, 170, 218

Coaching, DIY Life, 81-91

Coeliac disease, 30

Coercion, 52

Coherence and incoherence, 160-161, 171-176, 215

Comfort zones, 119-129

Communicating, 38-39, 63-69, 89

body language, 6, 38, 48, 63, 67-68

 non-verbally, 67

Conditioning, 106, 109, 123, 144,

Confirmation bias, 146-148

Conventional medicine, 169

Covey, Stephen, 65, 127, 260, 263

Craig, Gary, 180, 268

Criticism, 43-45, 47, 90, 189

Cyberbullying, 54-55

Cycle of Change, 116, 126, 129


**D**

Darwin, Charles, 151

Dawson, Karl, 203, 239, 253, 269

Deposits, emotional, 65-66

Disclaimer, iii

Dispenza, Dr Joe, 124-125, 130, 161, 253, 255, 260-268

Double bind, 54-55

Distorted belief, 78

DNA, 104, 151-155, 208, 224

Watson and Crick, 151

Dopamine, 25


**E**

E + R = O, 67, 79, 218

Early development, 97, 100

Early Learning, 97, 233

ECHO, 203-212

EFT, 177, 203-212

Einstein, 82, 149

Electromagnetic field, 171

Emotional Bank Account, 65

Emotional brain, 10-11, 66, 126, 133, 141

Emotional freedom technique, See EFT

Empathy, 10, 82, 140

Energy psychology, 82, 169, 172, 176, 180, 235-236,

Epigenetics, 154-155, 161, 224, 269

Erikson, 97

Exercise, 15, 16, 20, 31, 152, 163, 177

**F**

Low fat, 26, 29

Feedback, 40, 42, 92, 107-117, 138-140, 162, 165, 175

Feinstein, David PhD, 178, 235

Felitti, Dr Vincent, 233

Fight, flight or freeze, 9-12, 69, 71, 178-179

First nature second nature, 3, 63, 124

Five-Second Rule, 232

Frankl, Viktor, Man's Search for Meaning, 132

Fuller, Buckminster, xi


**G**

Galton, Sir Francis, 151-152

Gastro intestinal tract, 18, 22, 25, 167, 221, 258,

Genes, 152-155

Genetic determinism, 151-152

Engineering, 152

Gluten, 22, 29-30, 166

Grooming, online, 55-57, 260

Groupthink, 147-150, 263-264

Gruder, David, 235

Guided imagery, 161, 163-164

Gut bacteria, 24

Microbiome, 23, 25

# H

Hanson, Dr Rick, 157-158, 231-232, 265

Healing, xi, x, 20, 26, 28, 61, 152, 162-169, 176, 178, 182, 191, 202, 203, 234-237

Heavy metals, 21

Hebb's Law, 66, 93, 104-105, 126

Holistic, 6, 15, 165

Human genome project, 153, 224

Hyman, Dr Mark, 19-20, 22, 238

Hypothesis, 97, 146-147, 156

# I

Imagination, 79, 140

Imprints, 175

Incoherence,160-161

Inflammatory disease, 22, 24, 26

Influencing, 41, 63, 151

Intergenerational inheritance, 208

Internal dialogue, 93, 116

Intuition, 92, 141

# J

Janis, 148

Johnson, Jenny, 239

Jung, Carl, 204

# K

Kaku, Michio, 3

Kerry Babies, 147

Kinesiology, 163, 179

King, larry, 236

King, Sharon, 208, 239

Kolb's Learning Cycle, 112-113


# L

Labelling, 29

Law of Repetition, 105

Leaky Gut, 22

Lee, John, The Anger Solution, 72

Lerner, Harriet, The Dance of Anger, 72

Lesser, Elizabeth, 213

Leyden, Dr Lori, Create Global Healing and Project Light Rwanda, 182

Lindenfield, Gael, 42

Lipton, Dr Bruce, 154-155, 253

Lock on/lock out principle, 146-148

Locus of Control, 35, 48


# M

Manipulation, 37, 52, 56-59, 163

Maslow's Hierarchy of Needs, 134-136

Matrix Birth Reimprinting, 208-209, 239

Matrix Reimprinting, 203-211, 227, 229, 239

Meditation, 31, 121, 161, 163, 178-179, 221, 232, 235

Mehrabian, 67

Memory loss, deterioration, 4, 17

Memory transference, 171

Mercury, 21

Meta-medicine, 77

Milieu intérieur, 151-155, 162

Mirror therapy, 175-176

Motivation, 93, 131-142, 166, 200

Human Givens, 136-137

inherent resources, 139

Needs and wants, 131

Robbins, Tony, 134-136, 217

Murphy Paul, Annie, 233


**N**

Nature vs Nurture, 151

Neurons, 3, 4, 66, 93, 100, 104, 122, 171, 176,

Neuroscience, xiii, 4, 15, 98, 232

Neurotransmitters, 18, 25, 68-69, 120, 155

NLP, 163


**O**

Observer self, 141-142, 223

Oliver, Jamie, 26

Organic produce, 27

Ortner, Jessica, 183, 197

Ortner, Nick, 181-183, 197

## P

Passive aggressive, 38-39

Passivity, 37-39, 99

Pasteur, Louis, 151

Pattern matching, 145

Personal baggage, 11, 78, 80

Personal boundaries, See Boundaries, personal 51-61, 220

Phantom limb, 175-176

Piaget, 97

Placebo and Nocebo 15, 109-110, 125, 150, 161, 170, 203, 253, 261

Planck, Max, 203

Pratt, Dr Georg, 236

Protocols, 183, 204, 206-207

Psychology, Energy, See Energy Psychology

PTSD, 76, 170, 182, 184, 189, 202, 207, 235

## Q

Quantum physics, xiii, 159

## R

Ramachandran, 175

Refined sugar, 22,26-28, 31

Reframing, 116, 149, 187, 204

Reiki, 163

Reilly, David, 236

Remission, 153, 162

Resnick, Dr Robert, 10

Robbins, Anthony, 134-136, 217

Rolfing, 163

Rotter, Dr Julian, 35

Rumsfeld, Donald, 146

Rules, 4, 61, 63, 74-75, 99, 103, 105-106, 128, 132, 148, 154


**S**

Sandy Hook Elementary School, 182

Scaer, Dr Robert, 76, 204

Schwartz, Arielle, Ph.D, 221

Seahorn, Janet, 234

Self-fulfilling prophecy, 111

Self-talk, 66-67, 148, 156, 162

Self-talk cycle, 111, 114, 129

Serotonin, 25

Shanahan, Professor Fergus, 24

Shawshank Redemption, 128

Shepherd, Janine, 236

Siegel Daniel, xii, 8, 219

Simonton, 163, 238

Social media, boundaries, 54-55

Spiritual, xii, xiii, 80, 132-133, 136, 138, 152, 170, 173, 213-225

Standard American Diet, 26

State of being, 124, 129

Stay Safe Programme, 55

Stress hormones, 68, 99, 121, 155, 179

# T

Tabula rasa, 97

Tai Chi, 163, 178

Tapping, See EFT

Tapping – developing the process, 194

Tapping, how to start, 190

Tapping points, 187-188

Tapping Reminder phrase, 190-197

Tapping – scoring, 193

Tapping – setup phrase, 191

Tapping Tree, 189-190 TCM, 177-178

Tapping – what to tap on, 191

TED Talks, xiii, 8, 231-239

Temperament, 155

Traditional Chinese Medicine, 177, 202

Trauma, and Anger, 71-80

Trauma Big T and Small t, 75-77, 175, 203, 207

Triangle of Well-being, xii

Trinity College Dublin, xii, 15

TCD Institute of Neuroscience, 15

Toxic stress, 73, 101

Tuerk, Peter, 234


# U

UDIN, 77, 79, 184, 207

University of California, San Francisco, 15

## V

Van der Kolk, Bessel, 234-235
Vaughn, Don, 232
Vibratory resonance, 174
Virtues Project, 40
Vygotsky, 97

## W

Wahls, Dr Terry, 162, 238
Western medicine, 178
Willpower, 112, 115, 125-126, 166
Wimberger, Lisa, 231

## Y

Yellow-card, 71, 80, 92, 107
Young, Robert, O, Ph.D, 30

# Bibliography

Beattie, Melody, Codependent No More, How to Stop Controlling Others and Start Caring for Yourself, 1986, 1992 by the Hazelden Foundation

Dawson, Karl and Allenby, Sasha, Matrix Reimprinting Usingwrite your past; transform your future, Hay House, 2010

Dawson, Karl and Marillat, Kate, Transform Your Beliefs, Transform Your Life, EFT Tapping Using Matrix Reimprinting, Hay House 2014

Dispenza, Dr Joe, You Are the Placebo, Making Your Mind Matter, Hay House Inc., 2014

Dispenza, Dr Joe., Breaking the Habit of Being Yourself, How to Lose Your Mind and Create a New One, Hay House, 2012

Gaffney, Maureen PhD, (2011), *Flourishing,* Penguin, Ireland

King, Sharon, Heal Your Birth, Heal Your Life, Tools to Transform your Birth experience and Create a Magical New Beginning, Silver-Wood Books, 2015

Lee, John, The Anger Solution, The Proven Method for Achieving Calm and Developing Healty, Long-Lasting Relationships, De Capo Press, a member of the Perseur Books Group, 2009

Lipton, Bruce H., PhD, The Biology of Belief, Unleashing the Power of Consciousness, Matter & Miracles, Hay House, 10th Anniversary Edition, © 2005

McCraty, Rollin PhD, Science of the Heart, Exploring the Role of the Heart in Human Performance, Volume 2, HeartMath Institute 2015

Siegel, Daniel, MD and Payne, Tina, PhD, The Whole-Brain Child, 12 Revolutionary Strategies to Nurture Your Child's Developing Mind, Bantam Books, 2012

Siegel, Daniel, Mindsight, Transform your brain with the new science of kindness, Oneworld Publications, London 2010

Young, Robert O, PhD., and Young, shelley Redford, The pH Miracle for Diabetes, The Revolutionary Lifestyle Plan for Type 1 and Type 1 Diabetes

,

# Endnotes

[1] Wikipedia [Internet] available from: https://en.wikipedia.org/wiki/Buckminster_Fuller

[2] Alzheimer Association [Internet], available from: www.alz.org/brain-tour/neuron_forest.asp

[3] Bruce H. Lipton, Ph.D., (2005), *The Biology of Belief - Unleashing the Power of Consciousness, Matter & Miracles,* Hay House

[4] Siegel, Daniel, M.D. and Bryson, Tina Payne, PhD., (2012), The Whole-Brain Child, 12 Revolutionary Strategies to Nurture Your Child's Developing Mind, USA

[5] National Institute of Mental Health, [Internet] published 2017, available from: https://www.nimh.nih.gov/health/educational-resources/brain-basics/brain-basics.shtm

[6] Trinity College Dublin [Internet], cited February 2014 available from: https://www.tcd.ie/news_events/articles/online-video-project-hopes-to-boost-ireland-s-brain-health/4555#.VLj3hks2ImE

[7] Trinity College Dublin [Internet], cited October 2016 available from: https://www.tcd.ie/Neuroscience/neil/resources/videos/hello-brain-films.php

[8] https://www.tcd.ie/Neuroscience/neil/resources/videos/hello-brain-films.php.

[9] https://www.tcd.ie/Neuroscience/neil/resources/videos/hello-brain-films.php

[10] Dispenza, J., (2014), You are the Placebo Making Your Mind Matter, Hay House

[11] Hyman, Mark Dr., [Internet video docu-series January 2018]

Episode 1: The Broken Brain Epidemic / MyStory , https://broken-brain.com/episode1/

[12] Science Daily, (2014), Surface area of the digestive tract much smaller than previously thought, source: University of Gothenburg, [Internet] available from: https://www.sciencedaily.com/releases/2014/04/140423111505.htm

[13] Enders, Dr Giulia, (2017), The surprisingly charming science of your gut, TEDX Danubia, published Nov 24, 2017, [Internet] available from: https://www.google.ie/search?q=The%20surprisingly%20charming%20science%20of%20your%20gut%20%20site%3Ayoutube.com&rlz=1C1DSGQ_enIE480IE548&oq=youtube&aqs=chrome..69i57j69i60l3j35i39j0.1415j0j8&sourceid=chrome&ie=UTF-8&ved=0ahUKEwiI8ZOrgKPbAhXMUlAKHdcjDbMQ2wEIMA&ei=lCAJW4jXKsylwQLXx7SYCw

[14] John Hopkins Medicine, accessed 24/01/2018 [Internet] The Brain-Gut Connection, https://www.hopkinsmedicine.org/health/healthy_aging/healthy_body/the-brain-gut-connection

[15] Integrative Psychiatry, Gut Brain dysfunction, [Internet] 24/01/2018, https://www.integrativepsychiatry.net/gut_brain_dysfunction.html-https://www.integrativepsychiatry.net/gut_brain_dysfunction.html

[16] Enders, Dr Giulia, (2017), The surprisingly charming science of your gut, TEDX Danubia, published Nov 24, 2017

[17] Hyman, Mark Dr., (2018), Episode 1: The Broken Brain Epidemic / MyStory

[18] Rosenberg, Gary A (2012), Neurological diseases in relation to the blood–brain barrier, J Cereb Blood Flow Metab. 2012 Jul; 32(7): 1139–1151. Published online 2012 Jan doi: 10.1038/jcbfm.2011.197, [Internet] https://www.ncbi.nlm.nih.gov/pmc/articles/PMC3390801/

[19] www.https://www.nobelprize.org/nobel_prizes/medicine/laureates/2017/press.html obelprize.org, (2017), Press Release, The

Nobel Prize in Physiology or Medicine 2017, [Internet] available from: https://www.nobelprize.org/nobel_prizes/medicine/laureates/2017/press.html

[20] Gómez-González B, Hurtado-Alvarado G, Esqueda-León E, Santana-Miranda R, Rojas-Zamorano JÁ, Velázquez-Moctezuma J., (2013), REM sleep loss and recovery regulates blood-brain barrier function, Current Neurovascular Research. 2013 Aug;10(3):197-207, [Internet] available from: https://www.ncbi.nlm.nih.gov/pubmed/23713739

[21] Maroon, Dr J, (2017) Square One, A Simple Guide to a Balanced Life,

[22] Hyman, Mark Dr., (2018) Episode 1: Broken Brain Epidemic/MyStory

[23] Health and Environment Alliance, (8 December 2016), [Internet] EU agrees dental amalgam ban in children, pregnant and breastfeeding women, http://www.env-health.org/resources/press-releases/article/eu-agrees-dental-amalgam-ban-in

[24] WHO Fact Sheet, Mercury and Health, 2017), [Internet] available from:      http://www.who.int/news-room/fact-sheets/detail/mercury-and-health

[25] Fasano, A, [Internet 24/01/2018], Zonulin, regulation of tight junctions, and autoimmune diseases, , Ann N Y Acad Sci. 2012 Jul; 1258(1): 25–33 , doi: 10.1111/j.1749-6632.2012.06538.x

[26] Bischoff, SC , Barbara, G, Buurman, W, Ockhuizen, T, Schulzke, J-D, Serino, M, Tilg H, Watson A, and Wells JM, (2014), Intestinal permeability – a new target for disease prevention and therapy, BMC Gastroenterol. 2014; 14: 189. Published online 2014 Nov 18. doi: 10.1186/s12876-014-0189-7. [Internet] available from: https://www.ncbi.nlm.nih.gov/pmc/articles/PMC4253991/

[27] Hyman, Mark Dr., (2018) Episode 1: Broken Brain Epidemic/MyStory

[28] WebMD, Inflammatory Bowel Disease, accessed May 2018, [Internet] available from: https://www.webmd.com/ibd-crohns-disease/inflammatory-bowel-syndrome#1

[29] Shanahan, Fergus, Professor, (2012), Microbes made me, The Royal Irish Academy, www.dublintalks.ie, www.youtube.com/watch?v=1yND6NjS9ss

[30] Knight, Rob, Professor, (2015), How our microbes make us who we are, TED Talks, [Internet] available at https://www.youtube.com/watch?v=i-icXZ2tMRM

[31] Interconnected, The Power to Heal from Within, (Nov-Dec 2018) hosted by Dr Pedram Shojai , 9-part online series

[32] Knight, Rob, Professor (2015), op.cit.

[33] Shanahan, Fergus, Professor, (2012), Microbes made me, The Royal Irish Academy, www.dublintalks.ie, www.youtube.com/watch?v=1yND6NjS9ss

[34] Shanahan, Fergus, Professor, (2012), ibid

[35] Knight, Rob, Professor, (2015) op.cit.

[36] Doe-Young Kim, MD, and Michael Camilleri, MD, (2000), Serotonin: A Mediator of the Brain–Gut Connection Gastroenterology Research Unit, Mayo Clinic and Mayo Foundation, Rochester, Minnesota, The American Journal of Gastroenterology Vol. 95, No. 10, 2000

[37] Bubenik GA. Gastrointestinal melatonin: localization, function, and clinical relevance, Dig Dis Sci Oct 2002:47(10), 2336-2348

[38] Mariotti, Ron, ND and Yarnell, Eric, ND, (2006), Melatonin and the Gut: The Untold Connection, ndnr Naturopathic Doctor News & Review, [Internet] available from: www.ndnr.com/pain-medicine/melatonin-and-the-gut-the-untold-connection/John Hopkins Medicine,

[39] Young, Robert O and Young, Shelley Redford, (2004), The pH Mirace for Diabetes, The Revolutionary Lifestyle Plan for Type 1 and Type 2 Diabetes, Piatkus, an imprint of Little, Brown Book Group, London

[40] Robbins, John and Ocean, (2017), The Real Food Action Guide, The Food Revolution Network, www.foodrevolution.org

[41] Greger, Michael MD, FACLM, (2017), Organic versus Conventional: Which has More Nutrients?, [Internet] available from nutritionfacts. org, https://nutritionfacts.org/2017/04/13/organic-versus-conventional-which-has-more-nutrients/

[42] Irish Organic Farmers & Growers Association, http://iofga.org/about/what-is-organic-food/

[43] Food Revolution Network, (2017), Eating the Rainbow: Why Eating a Variety of Fruits and Vegetables Is Important for Optimal Health, Food and Health, December 8, 2017, [Internet] available from: https://foodrevolution.org/blog/eating-the-rainbow-health-benefits/

[44] World Health Organisation, (updated 2017), 10 Facts on Obesity, [Internet] available from: http://www.who.int/features/factfiles/obesity/en/

[45] Cordain, L, Eaton, SB, Sebastian , A, Mann, N, Lindeberg, S, Watkins, BA, O'Keefe, JH, Brank-Miller, J, (2005), Origins and evolution of the Western diet: health implications for the 21st century, American Society for Clinical Nutrition,[Internet] http://ajcn.nutrition.org/content/81/2/341.short

[46] Medical Definition of Lifestyle Diseases, [Internet] https://www.medicinenet.com/script/main/art.asp?articlekey=38316

[47] Hyman, Mark Dr., (2018) Episode 1: Broken Brain Epidemic/MyStory

[48] [Internet] available from: http://www.wisdomcommons.org/virtue/9-assertiveness/quotes

[49] Lindenfield, Gael, (1993), Managing Anger, Dealing Positively with Hurt and Frustration, Thorsons, an imprint of HarperCollinsPublishers

[50] Sarah Barns For Mailonline, [Internet] cited 7 December 2015, available from: www.dailymail. co.uk/femail/article-3349378/How-National-Crime-Agency-brought-Bahraini-paedophile-ring-justice.html#ixzz4AJtdEAO0

[51] Webster, Emma Sarran, (2017), What Is Sexual Grooming? 7 Things to Know About This Abuse Tactic, [Internet] available from: https://www.allure.com/story/what-is-sexual-grooming-abuse

[52] Beattie, Melanie, (1992), Codependent No More, How to Stop Controlling Others and Start Caring for Yourself, Hazelden, USA

[53] Covey, Stephen R, (1997), The 7 Habits of Highly Sucessful Families, Simon & Schuster UK Ltd

[54] Gaffney, Maureen, Dr (2011), Flourishing, Penguin, Ireland

[55] Wikipedia, Hebbian Theory, [Internet] available from: https://en.wikipedia.org/wiki/Hebbian_theory

[56] Baumeister, R. F., Bratslavsky, E., Finkenauer, C., & Vohs, K., D. (2001). Bad is stronger than good. Review of General Psychology, 5(4), 323-370. doi: 10.1037//1089-2680.5.4.323

[57] Seligman, Martin, (2011), Flourish – A New Understanding of Happiness and Well-being and How to Achieve Them, Nicholas Brealing Publishing, London

[58] Cuddy, Amy, TED Talk 2012, [Internet], available from: https://www.ted.com/speakers/amy_cuddy

[59] Dispenza, Joe, (2012), Breaking the Habit of Being Yourself, How to Lose Your Mind and Create a New One, Hay House

[60] Dispenza, Dr Joe, (2014),You are the Placebo – Making Your Mind Matter, Hay House

[61] Lee, John, (2009),The Anger Solution, De Capo Press, Cambridge, Massachusetts

[62] Diagnostic and Statistical Manual of Mental Disorders, The American Psychiatric Association

[63] Siegel, Daniel J and Solomon, Marion, Editors, (2003), Healing Trauma: Attachment, Mind, Body and Brain Norton Series on Interpersonal Neurobiology, W.W. Norton & Company, Inc, NY

[64] Scaer, Robert C, MD, Observations on Traumatic Stress Utilizing the Model of the "Whiplash Syndrome" , [Internet], available from: http://www.traumasoma.com/excerpts/Observations

[65] Meta-Health International Conference 2014, Tap Into Wellbeing, [Internet], available from: http://tapintowellbeing.com/tag/meta-health/

[66] Whitworth, Laura and Kimsey-House, Henry, (1995), Co-active Coaching: New Skills for Coaching People Toward Success in Work and Life, Nicholas Brealey Publishing

[67] McLeod, S, (2012), [Internet], Developmental Psychology, availablefrom: https://www.simplypsychology. org/developmental-psychology.html

[68] Dispenza, Dr Joe, (2012), Breaking the Habit of Being Yourself, Hay House

[69] Kirkpatrick, CM, (1999), [Internet], When Does Learning Begin? An Inquiry Into Fetal Cognition. A Senior Thesis In General Studies, College of Arts and Sciences, Texas Tech University, Department of Psychology, available from: https://ttu-ir.tdl.org/ttu-ir/bitstream/handle/2346/23168/31295013633416.pdf?sequence=1

[70] Morgan, Nicola, (2007), Know Your Brain, Walker Books, London

[71] Dispenza, Joe, op. cit.

[72] ACES Study, Center for Disease Control & Prevention, [Internet], Injury Prevention & Control: Division of Violence Prevention,

available from: https://www.cdc.gov/violenceprevention/acestudy/about.html

[73] ACES Study ibid

[74] ACES Study ibid

[75] University of Arizona, Tucson, author unstated, [Internet], Evaluating the National Outcomes, Parent and Family, available from: https://cals.arizona.edu/sfcs/cyfernet/nowg/pf_parent_nurture.html

[76] Encyclopedia of World Biography [Internet], Oprah Winfrey Biography, available from: http://www.notablebiographies.com/We-Z/Winfrey-Oprah.html

[77] Encyclopedia of World Biography [Internet], Bill Clinton Biography, available from: https://www.biography.com/people/bill-clinton-9251236

[78] Encyclopedia of World Biography [Internet], Barack Obama Biography, available from: http://www.notablebiographies.com/news/Li-Ou/Obama-Barack.html

[79] Encyclopedia of World Biography [Internet], Saddam Hussein Biography, available from: http://www.notablebiographies.com/news/Ge-La/Hussein-Saddam.html

[80] Nimi, Maj-Britt, (2009), Scientific American, February 2009, Volume 20, Issue 1, Placebo Effect: A Cure in the Mind [Internet], available from: https://www.scientificamerican.com/magazine/mind/2009/02-01/

[81] Placebo-controlled study, Wikipedia, [Internet] available from: https://en.wikipedia.org/wiki/Placebo-controlled_study

[82] Barber, Nigel, PhD., (2012), Voodoo Death 1- Hex death is not restricted to tribal societies - it may visit hospitals ..., Psychology Today, 10 Sep 2012, [Internet] available from https://www.psychologytoday.com/us/blog/the-human-beast/201209/voodoo-death-i

[83] University of Leicester, [Internet] http://www2.le.ac.uk/departments/gradschool/training/eresources/teaching/ theories/kolb

[84] Taylor, Ros, (2005), The Complete Mind Makeover, Transform your life and achieve success, Kogan Page London

[85] Dispenza, Joe, Dr (2014), You are the Placebo, Making your Mind Matter, Hay House

[86] Edelman, Ric, Chairman and CEO of Edelman Financial Services LLC, [Internet], Why So Many Lotttery Winners Go Broke, available from: http://fortune.com/2016/01/15/powerball-lottery-winners/

[87] Dispenza, J., (2012), Breaking the Habit of Being Yourself, Hay House.

[88] Covey, Stephen R, (1997), The 7 Habits of Highly Effective Families, Simon & Schuster

[89] Spratt, Eve G. MD, MSCR, Friedenberg, Samantha L.BS, Swenson, Cynthia C. PhD, LaRosa, Angela MD, MSCR, De Bellis, Michael D. MD, Macias, Michelle M. MD, Summer, Andrea P. MD, Hulsey, Thomas C. MSPH, ScD, Runyan, Des K. MD, PhD, and Brady, Kathleen T MD, PhD, (2012), The Effects of Early Neglect on Cognitive, Language, and Behavioral Functioning in Childhood, Psychology (Irvine). 2012 Feb 1; 3(2): 175–182, [Internet] available from: https://www.ncbi.nlm.nih.gov/pmc/articles/PMC3652241/

[90] The Human Givens Institute, [Internet], available from: http://www.hgi.org.uk/human-givens-essentials

[91] The Human Givens Institute ibid

[92] Lipton, B, PhD, (2015), The Biology of Belief, Unleashing the Power of Consciousness, Matter & Miracles, Hay House

[93] Janis, Irving L. (1972). Symptoms of Groupthink, Victims of Groupthink. , New York: Houghton Mifflin [Internet], available from http://www.psysr.org/about/pubs_resources/groupthink%20overview.htm

[94] Psychologists for Social Responsibility, [Internet], available from:

http://www.psysr.org/about/pubs_resources/groupthink%20over-view.htm

[95] Lipton, Bruce H., PhD., (2005), The Biology of Belief, Unleashing the Power of Consciousness,Matter & Miracles, Hay House Inc.

[96] Wikipedia, [Internet], available from: https://en.wikipedia.org/wiki/Claude_Bernard

[97] Bedson, J, MBChB, MRCGP, GP Research Fellow, McCarney, Rob, MPhil, Research Associate, Croft, Peter, MD, Professor of Epidemiology, Labelling chronic illness in primary care: a good or a bad thing?, British Journal of General Practice, Br J Gen Pract. 2004 Dec 1; 54(509): 932–938.

[98] National Human Genome Research Institute, What is the Human Genome Project? [Internet], https://www.genome.gov/11511417/what-is-the-human-genome-project/

[99] NIH, National Human Genome Research Institute, International Human Genome Sequencing Consortium Announces "Working Draft" of Human Genome, June 2000, [Internet], https://www.genome.gov/10001457/2000-release-working-draft-of-human-genome-sequence/

[100] Lipton, Bruce H., PhD, The Biology of Belief, Unleashing the Power of Consciousness,Matter & Miracles, Hay House Inc.

[101] Oschman, James, (2015), Energy Medicine: The Scientific Basis and Energy Medicine in Therapeutics, Churchill Livingstone, London, England

[102] Lipton, Bruce H. and Bhaerman, Steve, (2011), Spontaneous Evolution, Our Positive Future (and a way to get there from here, Hay House

[103] National Human Genome Research Institute, What is the Human Genome Project?

[104] Dispenza, Joe, (2012), op. cit.

[105] Dispenza, J. (2014), op. cit.

[106] Lipton, Bruce H, Dr and Bhaerman, Steve, Dr (2011), Spontaneous Evolution, Our Positive Future, Hay House

[107] Hanson, Rick, (2013), Hardwiring Happiness: Dr. Rick Hanson at TEDxMarin 2013, [Internet] available from: https://www.youtube.com/watch?v=jpuDyGgIeh0

[108] Dispenza, J. (2014), op. cit.

[109] Oschman, James, (2015), Energy Medicine: The Scientific Basis and Energy Medicine in Therapeutics, Churchill Livingstone, London, England

[110] Oschman James, Energy Research US, [Internet], http://www.energyresearch.us

[111] Dispenza, Joe, Dr (2014), op.cit.

[112] Gelles, David, (2015), Mindful Work, How Meditation is Changing Business from the Inside Out, Profile Books Ltd., 3 Holford Yard, Bevin Way, London WC1X 9HD

[113] Dispenza, J. (2012) op. cit.

[114] Wark, Chris, www.chrisbeatcancer.com

[115] Wahls, Dr Terry, (2015) , How I Went From Wheelchair To Walking By Changing My Diet, [Internet] available from: https://www.youtube.com/watch?v=lJT4gRUlpkc

[116] Nerenberg, Bev, accessed 2017, EFT Instruction Given at Hospital Ranked 4th Best in US, [Internet] available from: http://www.eftuniverse.com/eft-workshops-and-training/eft-instruction-given-at-hospital-ranked-4th-best-in-us

[117] Simonton, O Carl MD, James Creighton PhD, Stephanie Matthews Simonton, (1978), Getting Well Again, Bantam Books

[118] Simonton, ibid

[119] Millman, Dan, (2000 Revised Edition), Way of the Peaceful Warrior, HJ Kramer, New World Library, Novato, California

[120] Roy, Vandana, Gupta, Monica and Kumar Ghosh, Raktim, (2015), Perception, attitude and usage of complementary and alternative medicine among doctors and patients in a tertiary care hospital in India, Indian Journal of Pharmacology, 2015 Mar-Apr; 47(2): 137–142. [Internet] available from: https://www.ncbi.nlm.nih.gov/pmc/articles/PMC4386119/

[121] Center for Integrative Medicine, University of Arizona, [Internet], https://integrativemedicine.arizona.edu/about/definition.html

[122] Zielinski, Eric DC., (2018), The Healing Power of Essential Oils, Harmony Books, New York

[123] Oschman, James L, Dr (2000), Energy Medicine, The Scientific Basis, Churchill Livingstone, an Imprint of Elsevier Limited

[124] Chen C. Will, Tai Chen-Jei, Choy Cheuk-Sing, Hsu Chau-Yun Shoei-Loong Lin, Chan, Wing P. Chan Chiang Han-Sun, Chen, Chang-An, and Leung Ting-Kai, (2013), Wave-Induced Flow in Meridians Demonstrated Using Photoluminescent Bioceramic Material on Acupuncture Points, Evidence Based Complementary and Alternative Medicine. 2013; 2013: 739293. [Internet] available from: https://www.ncbi.nlm.nih.gov/pmc/articles/PMC3838801/

[125] [Internet] The 7 Chakras – A Beginners Guide To Your Energy System, available from https://www.zenlama.com/the-7-chakras-a-beginners-guide-to-your-energy-system/

[126] The Human Energy System: The Aura, Subtle Bodies & Chakras, [Internet] available from: https://www.crystalherbs.com/chakras-subtle-bodies.asp

[127] Braden, Gregg, (2015), Resilience from the Heart – the power to thrive in life's extremes, Hay House

[128] ibid

[129] The British Heart Foundation [Internet] available from: https://www.bhf.org.uk/heart-health/treatments/heart-transplant

[130] European Commission Report (2014), Journalist Workshop on Organ donation and transplantation Recent Facts & Figures, 26 November 2014 – Brussels, Source: 2013 and 2014 Transplant Newsletters, Global Observatory on Donation & Transplantation, [Internet] available from: https://ec.europa.eu/health/sites/health/files/blood_tissues_organs/docs/ev_20141126_factsfigures_en.pdf

[131] Braden, Gregg, op. cit.

[132] McCraty, Rollin PhD, (2015), Science of the Heart, Exploring the Role of the Heart in Human Performance, Volume 2, HeartMath Institute

[133] McCraty, ibid

[134] Laser, accessed April 2018, [Internet] available at https://en.wikipedia.org/wiki/Laser

[135] Heitler, S, PhD, (2012), [Internet], Can Energy Psychology Treatments End Chronic Pain?, available from: [www.psychologytoday.com/blog/resolution-not-conflict/201206/can-energy-psychology-treatments-end-chronic-pain

[136] Radcliffe Shawn (2014), [Internet], For Pain Patients, the Physical and Emotional Are Intertwined, available from: http://www.healthline.com

[137] BBC2 Series, Incredible Medicine; Dr Weston's Casebook, March 2017

[138] Sae Young Kim, MD and Yun Young Kim, MD, Mirror Therapy for Phantom Limb Pain, Korean Journal of Pain, 2012 Oct; 25(4): 272–274, published online available from: https://doi.org/10.3344/kjp.2012.25.4.272

[139] Feinstein, David, PhD, (2010), The Case for Energy Psychology – Snake Oil or Designer Tool for Change?, Psychotherapy Networker Magazine, [Internet] available from: http://www.innersource.net/ep/images/stories/downloads/PN_article.pdf

[140] Feinstein, David, PhD, Tapping World Summit Interview, (2012), [Internet] available from: https://www.thetappingsolution.com/science-research/

[141] Healthcare Medicine Institute, (2014), Acupuncture For Military PTSD Found Effective, 19 December 2014, [Internet], available at: http://www.healthcmi.com/Acupuncture-Continuing-Education-News/1410-acupuncture-for-combat-ptsd-found-effective

[142] Dispenza, J. (2014), op. cit.

[143] Clond, M (2016), [Internet], Emotional Freedom Techniques for Anxiety: A Systematic Review With Meta-analysis, Journal of Nervous & Mental Disease . 204(5):388-395, May 2016, available from: https://www.ncbi.nlm.nih.gov/pubmed/26894319

[144] [Internet] available from: http://www.rogercallahan.com/callahan.php

[145] Feinstein, D, Eden, D and Craig, G, (2005), The Promise of Energy Psychology, Jeremy P Tarcher/Penguin

[146] Swingle, PG, Pulos, L, Swingle, MK, [Internet], Neurophysiological Indicators Of Eft Treatment Of Post-Traumatic Stress, Subtle Energies &Energy Medicine,Volume15, Number 1, 2005 available from: http://scholar.google.com/scholar_url?url=http://journals.sfu.ca/seemj/index.php/seemj/article/download/

[147] Zimmerman, R (2013), [Internet]Trauma Update: On The 'Tipping Point For Tapping' Therapy, available from: https://hms.harvard.edu/news/trauma-update-tipping-point-tapping-therapy-7-23-13

[148] Marchant, J. (2016), [Internet], Cure: A Journey Into The Science of Mind Over Body, available at:

[149] Swingle et al. ibid

[150] Church, Dr D,Hawk, C, Brooks, A J, Toukolehto, O, Wren, M, Dinter, I, Stein, P. [Internet],Psychological Trauma Symptom Improvement in Veterans Using Emotional Freedom Techniques: A Randomized Controlled Trial, Journal of Nervous & Mental Disease: February 2013, Volume 201 - Issue 2 - p 153–160

[151] Dr Lori Leyden, Project Light [Internet], available from: https://www.createglobalhealing.org/

[152] EFT for War Veterans with PTSD by EFT Tapping, [Internet] available from: https://www.youtube.com/watch?v=B4hhMm8qsCs

[153] Church, Dawson, Dr (2016), The Epigenetics of the Matrix from Cell to Cosmos, Matrix Summit 2016

[154] Braden, Gregg, (2016), Resilience from the Heart, Hay House, Inc.

[155] Braden, Gregg, (2007), The Divine Matrix, Hay House, Inc.

[156] Radford, John and Govier, Ernest, Editors, (1980), A Textbook of Psychology, Sheldon Press

[157] Brouwer, J.R, (2012),[Internet], A Crash Course in Epigenetics Part 1: An intro to epigenetics, available from: http://bitesizebio.com/8807/a-crash-course-in-epigenetics-part-1-an-intro-to-epigenetics/

[158] Siegel, Daniel, (2011), Mindsight, Transform your Brain with the New Science of Kindness, A Oneworld Book, Great Britain

[159] From Spirit Voyage website, adapted by Arielle Swartz, PhD, and reproduced with permission [Internet] available from: http://drarielleschwartz.com/trauma-legacies-and-transgenerational-healing-dr-arielle-schwartz/#.WDQdLixvh2Y